TRUST BETRAYED:
Inside the AARP

TRUST BETRAYED:
Inside the AARP

By **DALE VAN ATTA**

REGNERY PUBLISHING, INC.
Washington, D.C.

Library of Congress Cataloging-in-Publication Data

Van Atta, Dale.
      Trust betrayed: inside the AARP / by Dale Van Atta.
         p.   cm.
      Includes bibliographical references and index.
      ISBN 0–89526–485–4
      1. American Association of Retired Persons—Corrupt practices.
2. Retirees—Societies, etc.—Corrupt practices—United States.
3. Pressure groups—Corrupt practices—United States. 4. Lobbying—Corrupt practices—United States. I. Title.
HQ1063.2.U6V37   1998
306.3'8'0973—dc21   97–49322
                                                CIP

Published in the United States by
Regnery Publishing, Inc.
An Eagle Publishing Company
One Massachusetts Avenue, N.W.
Washington, DC 20001

Distributed to the trade by
National Book Network
4720-A Boston Way
Lanham, MD 20706

Printed on acid-free paper.
Manufactured in the United States of America

Design by Kristine Lund

10 9 8 7 6 5 4 3 2 1

Books are available in quantity for promotional or premium use. Write to Director of Special Sales, Regnery Publishing, Inc., One Massachusetts Avenue, N.W., Washington, DC 20001, for information on discounts and terms or call (202) 216-0600.

By the same author:

STORMIN' NORMAN: AN AMERICAN HERO

To my intrepid mother,
Vera Van Atta,
for her many talents,
insight, love,
unquestioning support, and
general joie de vivre.

CONTENTS

TRUST BETRAYED:
Inside the AARP

Chapter 1

Taking the Public to the Cleaners

> If it were a sovereign nation of old people, the AARP would be the 31st-largest country in the world.
>
> *—Orlando Sentinel-Tribune*

> AARP advocated more than 100 ideas for new spending that within a decade would cause annual federal outlays to rise by more than $1 trillion.
>
> *—Paul Hewitt, former executive director of the National Taxpayers Union Foundation*

With its thirty-three million–strong membership, the American Association of Retired Persons (AARP) is the second-largest organization in the United States, after the Catholic Church. When the AARP lobbies Congress, which it spends much of its time and huge budget doing, it claims to do so for half the senior citizens of the United States. But all too often, the AARP actively promotes causes seniors neither like nor find beneficial. Some even run counter to their interests, especially the AARP's relentless support of ever higher taxes, disastrous health care legislation that threatens seniors, and a whole litany of other liberal causes (such as attempting to defeat the nomination of Clarence Thomas to the Supreme Court). These efforts are subsidized by the AARP's numerous business enterprises, including insurance and pharmaceuticals, which the AARP claims are a nonprofit service to seniors, but which are really a revenue engine for the AARP and a profit engine for its business partners.

This isn't the way it was supposed to be. The AARP was founded by Ethel Percy Andrus, a retired schoolteacher who envisioned a non-partisan service organization dedicated to lending dignity to old age.

Andrus was herself a conservative Republican steeped in the American ethos of God, country, and self-reliance. She explicitly stated that the "*AARP is not a pressure group, petitioning for special privileges and exemptions because of age and numbers.*" Two decades later those noble thoughts were translated by an AARP staffer as: "Our ideology is 'big.'"

"Big" the AARP certainly is... big and arrogant. According to AARP Executive Director Horace Deets the AARP is not a typical charitable organization—its aims are too big. He suggests it has to be run, at least in part, like a business: "Given our size, you cannot run this like a bake sale after Church on Sunday."[1] But that raises an obvious question. If the AARP is a business, why isn't it taxed as any other business would be? In the 1980s, the Internal Revenue Service (IRS), in fact, asked a similar question, demanding hundreds of millions of dollars in back taxes from the AARP. After nearly a decade, the AARP finally coughed up $135 million, which in the AARP's Orwellian words, were paid "in lieu of taxes." According to AARP sources, that was *less than a fourth* of what the IRS claimed the AARP actually owed. Really, all that distinguishes the AARP from most profit-making businesses is that it is *big* business (its flagship magazine, *Modern Maturity*, has a bigger circulation than *Time*, *Newsweek*, and *U.S. News & World Report* combined). And it is big business subsidized by the taxpayer through the huge tax loophole of the AARP's officially being a nonprofit organization.

The AARP does many things—from selling insurance to endorsing products—on a massive scale. Its sheer size is intimidating, its budget enormous. In 1993 and 1994, AARP's revenue was around

$470 million. Less than half of that comes from membership dues. A hefty chunk of it comes from you and me, the American taxpayers, in the form of federal funding. In 1993, the last year for which figures are available, the AARP received $86 million (or nearly 20 percent of its operating costs) from the federal government. In addition to federal grants, the AARP receives special nonprofit rates from the U.S. Postal Service—a rate they sometimes abuse for unjustifiable purposes. Former U.S. Senator Alan Simpson charged, for instance, that "the AARP saved, and the taxpayers paid, more than $5 million in 1991 and 1992 by [the AARP's] improperly mailing health insurance solicitations at nonprofit rates."

Secret health task force documents released under threat of a lawsuit indicate that the AARP actually helped design the Clinton Health Care Plan—a plan its own members didn't want.

WHAT DO SENIORS get for the money they spend on dues and taxpayers spend on their behalf through federal subsidies? One celebrated example was given in the June 1992 issue of *The Washington Monthly* by Christopher Georges, who tried to trace the $75 million the AARP gets to run job training and job placement programs for older citizens. Georges's quest proved futile:

> Jack Everett, an official in the organization's Senior Employment Office… cheerfully explained that the AARP offers no federally funded job placement or training programs. Everett suggested calling the Department of Labor (the agency that pays the AARP $52 million to run one of the programs) for help. He also offered other ideas, like "Try the phone book under the senior citizens' section," and suggested contacting the National Council of Senior Citizens, another smaller advocacy group for older Americans. He even threw in some job-training advice: "You'll need a resume. That's always a good first step…."

But the industrious Georges didn't stop with the Washington headquarters; he called branch offices. "Similar inquiries at AARP offices in major cities in sixteen states turned up similar responses:

Only six of the officers were aware that these programs exist, although the AARP literature boasts that they're offered at 108 sites across the nation. One office suggested calling Elder Temps, a privately run job-placement firm. Another advised calling the Jewish Council for the Aging. Several others suggested enrolling in an AARP job search workshop and seminar—for a fee of $35.

Perhaps the AARP's excuse for this ignorance is that its officers are too busy lobbying for yet more tax dollars. The AARP's dependence on federal largesse has made it an active lobbyist for ever-higher taxes and entitlement spending. The AARP's magisterial 462-page agenda, *Toward a Just and Caring Society*, says that the association's "highest priority" is "raising taxes on the highest income taxpayers." The AARP has also called for higher gasoline, alcohol, and other consumer taxes. When it comes to taxes, the AARP wants them all. How do we balance the budget? Well, we raise taxes. Needless to say, the AARP is a fervent foe of cutting the capital gains tax (a tax cut that especially benefits elderly investors who want to cash out and live off their earnings). Somewhat ironically in light of its own run-in with the tax man, the AARP has a high regard for the IRS, asserting that there should be more IRS audits (presumably for thee and me rather than the AARP). To attain this goal, the AARP proposes that the IRS's "examination and enforcement staffs should be increased." One wonders how many elderly Americans agree with this, hoping that the IRS will come knocking at their, or their children's, or their grandchildren's doors.

But one doesn't have to wonder long. For when it comes to choosing between the interests of seniors and the interests of big government—the big government that feathers the AARP's nest— big government wins every time.

For example, in 1988, the AARP was a vigorous supporter of the Catastrophic Health Care Act, which would have cost many senior citizens an additional $800 a year in taxes. When senior citizens realized the bill's financial impact, there was a historic revolt of the AARP's rank and file. In a highly unusual reversal, Congress repealed the act. As Hank Cox noted in *Regardie's* magazine, "The

American Association of Retired Persons may be the only lobby in Washington, D.C., with enough clout to bulldoze a massive new benefit program through the Congress, only to have its own members force the repeal of the program less than one year later, and not experience so much as a twinge of embarrassment or offer a hint of an apology."

The AARP was also a major booster of the ill-fated Clinton health care reform package, despite an overwhelmingly negative response from senior citizens. In fact, secret health task force documents released under threat of a lawsuit indicate that the AARP actually helped design the Clinton Health Care Plan—a plan its own members didn't want. One document noted that "John Rother, AARP's legislative and public policy director, helped the administration draft a health-care reform bill to [the AARP's] liking." Arizona Senator John McCain, testifying before a Senate subcommittee, asserted that the AARP's mail-order prescription business stood to benefit from the Clinton plan.

For the innocent elderly who look to the AARP to defend seniors' interests, I have a simple message: Your trust has been betrayed.

That would not be surprising, because the AARP is a champion at defending its own—if not necessarily its members'—interests. It is certainly far, far removed from the disinterested organization visualized by its founder. And it is certainly far, far removed from the homey image it tries to project of being the best friend of the elderly.

Instead, the AARP is interested in churning money—enough to pay for its grandiose, marble-and-stone, $17 million-a-year headquarters; for the enormous six-figure salaries of its top executives; and for its feared lobbyists who raid the taxpayers' wallets without a thought as to who will inherit the bill for ever-more-expensive senior programs and entitlements.

Indeed, why should the AARP care about the bill when they don't even care about the federal programs—except insofar as they benefit the association? As we will see in the pages that follow, the AARP thinks of the elderly as sheep to be sheared, as a voting block to be manipulated, as volunteers to be used. And when the elderly fail to serve any profit-making purpose, the AARP is content to show them the door, and even discriminate against them.

For the innocent elderly who look to the AARP to defend seniors' interests, I have a simple message: Your trust has been betrayed.

Chapter 2

Out with the Old: Age Discrimination at AARP

> My wife and I are both 79 and we were members for a
> number of years before we dropped out. I think AARP
> stinks. They pay $17 million to rent a building in D.C.
> and then hire all young people to run it.
>
> *—Homer V. Lord, former AARP member,*
> *Kane, Pennsylvania*[1]

> I'm just an old bag that they trot out every time they
> have to show they have somebody old working for the
> Association.
>
> *—Lee Pearson, seventy-five-year-old AARP*
> *staffer in a remark to a fifty-eight-*
> *year-old staff colleague*

Few organizations have fought age discrimination as forcefully as
the AARP; few have testified more about it in Congress; few have
done more studies; and no association has joined or instigated more
lawsuits against large corporations who dare to degrade, demote, or
retire a valued employee simply because he or she has gotten older.

"Ever since AARP's founder, Dr. Ethel Percy Andrus, first spoke
out against age discrimination in employment more than 30 years
ago, we have been an advocate for the nation's growing number of
older workers," declares Executive Director Horace Deets. "We have
a right—and a *duty* —to speak out."[2]

AARP was instrumental in securing passage of the landmark Age Discrimination in Employment Act (ADEA) in 1967. AARP attorneys have initiated or participated in high-profile class action age discrimination suits against companies like Farmers Group (insurance company), Dresser Industries, and State Farm Insurance Companies.

Ironically, the organization that preaches against age discrimination practices it. It is the Achilles heel of AARP.

The AARP has been careful never to reveal to its members how many older employees it has. This was an organization once run entirely by retired persons, but now 80 percent of the AARP's staff are too young to qualify for AARP membership—fourteen percent are identified as between fifty-one and sixty years old, and only 6 percent are sixty-one or older. AARP member Palmer Payne of Boothbay Harbor, Maine, believes the Association's practice is shameful on this score:[3] "Curious as to AARP's true commitment to the elderly, I inquired a few years ago about the ages of the employees who write, edit, and publish the magazines and newsletters. The response was vague and non-responsive, saying people are hired on 'merit' rather than with consideration for age. This seems somewhat hypocritical—to operate a major lobbying effort against ageism in hiring and forced retirement; but not taking a more affirmative stand internally. They don't practice what they preach! I suspect AARP operates in *spite* of its members more than in *behalf* of them."

Age discrimination at AARP is evident in the *AARP Workforce Diversity Initiative*. This exhaustive two-year internal survey was launched by Horace Deets after staff members charged that racial discrimination was widespread at AARP. Deets's attempt to be politically correct backfired when other minority groups complained that they were not included in the study. Deets then expanded the survey to include all "groups" at AARP but still failed to include any questions on age discrimination—the subject on which it is supposed to be the country's foremost expert.

One sixty-plus female AARP staffer commented on the initial survey: "I started working for AARP when Dr. Andrus was here. I've taken all the training I could get to keep up with changes, but I think they just don't want us older folk around any more; especially me, because I'm so outspoken. An older male AARP staffer concurs: "I'm old now and am afraid of losing my job.... There aren't many jobs today for equipment operators like me. And I'm not as strong as I used to be. I keep hearing rumors about all the jobs here being relocated or contracted out. I know I won't find another job if this place shuts down."

Tenaciously lobbied, AARP executives finally and quietly added the term "age" to its lists of diversity groupings on the final survey questionnaire.

The organization that preaches against age discrimination practices it.

Ultimately, 1,334 staffers filled out the eighteen-page discrimination questionnaire—a response rate of 78 percent. The survey found that many staffers felt discriminated against at AARP. Most astonishing, many experienced discrimination because of their age.

AARP leadership was so disturbed by the survey results that they buried or eliminated the findings, and stamped many survey-related reports "Confidential," restricting access to less than two dozen employees. When staffers were asked to comment on why the diversity study was initiated in the first place, many felt it was a way for AARP to avoid potential legal and financial ramifications from AARP staff discrimination lawsuits.

The diversity survey did not however stop Otis Gabriel, an eleven-year AARP veteran, from filing a lawsuit. Ironically, Gabriel served as Employee Relations Chief; during much of his career, his job was to instruct association employees about age, race, and sex discrimination.

In 1994, despite a plethora of good or outstanding performance reviews, the AARP "reassigned" the fifty-four-year-old Gabriel to head "Special Projects," a made-up Human Resources Department position designed to shift him away from the flow of operations. Typical of AARP older employee demotions, he did not lose his manager status, nor was there a loss in salary. "They know that you don't turn around and terminate an older employee," said Gabriel's lawyer, Bryan Chapman. "What you do is, you simply reduce their responsibilities or demote them, put them in a position where they decide on their own to retire or to resign."

AARP did defend itself by saying it had not demoted Gabriel, because he still had his title and salary. Rejoined Chapman: "Psychologically, if you take somebody who really had a high-visibility, high-responsibility job, like Otis Gabriel, and you do that to him, it doesn't matter whether you give him a nice office, keep him at a manager's title, and give him the same salary. The bottom line is that he knows that he's been demoted. He knows that he has lost face. And the effect can be even more devastating. It sets a guy like that up for ridicule. Among his colleagues, he's saying, Why am I excluded from meetings? Why is it that everybody has a secretary? I have no secretary; I have no staff; I have no budget; I have no defined duties; I'm not even on the organizational chart. Psychologically, you're sending this guy signals that say, 'It's time for you to go.'"

Gabriel got the message and was angry. "It seems so ironic," he later told one reporter.[4] "You'd think they would be more sensitive to age discrimination." Still, Gabriel had seen it happen to others at AARP and was not going to take it. So he filed suit in March 1996 in U.S. District Court in Washington, D.C., asking for $2 million in damages. Afterwards, he was ostracized at work; his desk was rifled in his absence; and he could no longer trust the phones to speak to friends because he was convinced they were tapped. No previous lawsuit had concerned AARP as much as this one. Gabriel was a respected executive who held a prominent position in the organization and knew the extent of employee discontent over discrimination and other issues.

"This is a bona fide case of age discrimination," Gabriel told a *Chicago Tribune* reporter.[5] "The reason I know it fits the definition is that AARP has a book that describes exactly what happened to me." In fact, he helped write AARP's age discrimination guidelines, including booklets passed out to corporations detailing the subtle and not-so-subtle signs by which an older employee may know he has suffered from such discrimination. Adds lawyer Chapman: "It was obvious that AARP was essentially phasing Gabriel out. They probably thought he'd get frustrated and leave on his own. But if you look at what the AARP advises older workers to look out for and take a look at what they did to my client, it's very clear that people who manage the organization have done something that clearly violates the policy of the organization."

AARP couldn't afford to have the Gabriel lawsuit go to court, so they offered an undisclosed cash settlement, which Gabriel accepted. He left AARP at the end of 1996, convinced that AARP knew it had a serious problem with age discrimination and was anxious to keep this covered up. He cannot speak about his case, because, as part of the settlement agreement, AARP required his silence.

This was an organization once run entirely by retired persons, but now 80 percent of the AARP's staff are too young to qualify for AARP membership.

The older employees seem to be bearing the brunt of AARP's recent restructuring and downsizing moves. In recent years, for instance, Deets has demoted three of his top longtime closest aides: Finance Division Director James Maigret, Strategic Planner Kirk Stromberg, and Chief of Staff Jim Ford. In the first two cases, they kept the same titles but had their authority curtailed and subordinated to younger employee replacements. Ford, considered quite capable for many years, was forced from the tenth floor to the third floor, where a new position was invented for him— "Director of Advocacy Training." His new, younger boss groused to a colleague that she might have had an opening for him "if I hadn't had Jim Ford dumped on me. I was told to take him, and that was that."

IN 1994 THE *AARP BULLETIN* RAN a front-page series bemoaning the fate of older workers who were "Downsized and Out." The *Bulletin* had requested firsthand stories and received more than ten thousand responses from members.

"Overwhelmingly," the AARP reported, "the replies paint a picture of forced retirements, frustrating and frequently unsuccessful efforts to find new employment, financial hardship and—sometimes—

dashed retirement hopes. Readers repeatedly cite questionable pressures being brought to bear to nudge, push, or otherwise propel them out the door. Of the 10,000 respondents, more than two-thirds indicated they left their jobs under duress, either involuntarily or voluntarily, but under pressure."

The *Bulletin* editors could have interviewed some of AARP's own current and ex-older employees and gotten the same responses. Even younger staff have realized what is happening. Consider these remarks appended to the diversity study:

> I think several retirees, who have been with the company over 20 years, felt pushed out subtly. They've taken their responsibilities away and were treated shabbily without regards to their contributions to the organization. They were given a beautiful retirement party, but it was hypocritical.

> When I worked in another division, a few more senior [employees] were sort of being pushed out the door slowly. They were being given fewer responsibilities until they got to the point where they decided that it wasn't worth being here. Just because a person is 75–80 does not mean that they can't think. It was pretty blatant. A lot of it had to do with the managers in charge, young blood coming in off of Capitol Hill. They think they are much more important than the rest of us.

GEORGE SUNDERLAND AND LEE PEARSON, both in their seventies, have run the Criminal Justice Services section of AARP for many years as manager and assistant manager, respectively. Both had remarkable backgrounds before AARP, were often awarded by outsiders and the association itself for their AARP work, and remain healthy and intellectually sharp. Their expertise is needed now more than ever, because crime against the elderly is a critical concern of AARP's membership. An interview I conducted with them was, up front, amicable and substantive. Both went out of their way to vouch for the AARP as a wonderful workplace for older employees.

Sunderland all but stood up and saluted the AARP flag. Pearson was less exclamatory, but still approving in her description of the AARP work environment.

Behind the scenes, the AARP was trying to eliminate their positions and create similar ones with altered job descriptions for which they might not qualify. Sunderland had been quietly storing away evidence he planned to use against the AARP should they suggest he leave. And Pearson, a witty, wonderful woman, was also convinced they were pressuring her to leave. She had grown tired, she said, of playing the token older employee at AARP events. She related that the AARP broadcast department was once finishing up a video for the members when they suddenly realized that everyone in the video was under thirty. Lee was importuned to come down, pose, and read some lines so the association wouldn't appear so young.

The AARP, in order to stifle harmful publicity, has settled many age discrimination lawsuits out of court and slapped a gag rule on the former or current employee.

"There have been lots of age discrimination suits at AARP," conceded one senior staffer. "But everybody signs a contract, and nobody says anything. They just give you a lot of money and you go away." AARP, in order to stifle harmful publicity, has settled many suits out of court and slapped a gag rule on the former or current employee. "AARP is an organization that says one thing and does another," said a sixty-plus highly regarded AARP employee who was demoted. "On the one hand, we have this big thing about older people, and how we respect them, and take care of them, and help them get jobs.... On the other hand, the association is throwing its older employees out on the street."

Chapter 3

This, That... and the Taj Mahal

The AARP is an organization that feathers its own nest in a not-too-shabby fashion. I recently saw its new headquarters building in Washington, D.C., which is 'top of the line.' God knows what it costs, but not too long ago I read it costs millions of dollars just to furnish it. Need I say that I recently canceled my AARP membership?

—*James Maas, Ph.D., Berkeley, California*[1]

Over $400 million a year in income, and they're supposed to be the nice guys. They know... that there isn't a politician in the country who would cut the benefits of poor older Americans, but these guys have become adept experts in squeezing the last five-dollar bill out of their purse.

—*Paul Hewitt, National Taxpayers Union Foundation*[2]

Where does the AARP spend its money? Well, for starters, on amenities such as its lavish headquarters, known as the Taj Mahal, and on generous salaries for the staff. Executive Director Horace Deets, for example, makes $287,000 a year, plus $49,000 in expenses. And Deets is not the only one. More than $83 million went for salaries and benefits in 1994. Nineteen of the AARP's 1,732 employees make more than $100,000 a year. And though the AARP's board—composed mostly of retired school teachers, administrators, and government workers—isn't paid, it does enjoy an array of perks, including travel and expense accounts, which in 1990, according to *The Washington Monthly*, totaled about *$11 million.*

And then there's the Taj Mahal…

If you want to get a concrete idea of the gulf that separates the AARP's leadership from the nation's elderly, go visit its magnificent, almost block-long building tucked away on Sixth and E Streets, N.W., Washington, D.C.

Elderly members are often put off by the edifice's obvious grandeur, but architectural critics tend to gush. As one of them put it, "the building draws its imagery from French and Italian neoclassicism, from ancient Greece and Rome, from the Renaissance genius of Palladio and the exuberant English mannerism of Sir Christopher Wren."

In addition to being beautiful, the headquarters is a "well building." "All of the materials, mechanical systems, and furnishings were carefully selected to avoid creating an environment conducive to the 'sick building syndrome,'" a staff memo noted. An expensive "bio-mechanical scientist" was hired as a special consultant to implement this wellness.

Several other well-paid consultants were brought in to scratch their heads over the proper colors needed "to produce an atmosphere conducive to a positive working environment, reflecting the people-oriented goals of the association." Marble plating, imported from Italy, is on each floor in green, white, red, and brown.

The lighting deserved equal scrutiny. "Lighting was considered from functional, aesthetic, and energy-saving points of view," informs the *Staff Information Handbook. Functional* means whatever the lighting committee/consultants thought worked. *Aesthetic* means soft lighting, including "a parabolic baffle to minimize both glare and veiling reflections." *Energy-saving* means low-watt bulbs and nifty new motion sensitive light switches. "No more groping for the light switch on your way in or out of your office!" the *Handbook* exults.

The AARP's twelve elevators are regulated by the computerized operations center on the roof, where the chief engineer can view each elevator's position. The AARP rooftop operations center also controls the temperature settings in the building—adjusting individual office thermostats, if requested. AARP's very own weather antennae on the roof peaks at 145 feet in the atmosphere. "It's got the wind speed, wind direction," an engineer ticks off. "It's got the vane anemometer, the temperature, humidity, ethyl P, wet bulb, solar intensity and so on." It controls the building's retractable awnings.

Security is heavy. The AARP has a staff of twenty guards and supervisors. Visitors pass through heavy bronze-clad steel outer and inner doors before getting to the security station, where they are inspected by a staffer and issued a pass. (Automatic inner/outer doors are available for the handicapped.) Two security stations are needed because the AARP building is technically two buildings connected by an impressive arcade/atrium that is covered by a pitched, glazed-roof structure.

If you want to get a concrete idea of the gulf that separates the AARP's leadership from the nation's elderly, visit its magnificent, almost block-long building tucked away on Sixth and E Streets, N.W.

All this doesn't come cheap. The annual rent is $16.75 million. At the Simpson hearings, the AARP tried to portray the building as really just about the least expensive available for a headquarters in Washington. The AARP's leadership has even implied that they had little to do with the construction or design of the building—it just sort of *happened* along the way.

The fact is, the AARP leadership was *intimately* involved with almost every phase of the construction and design. A close examination of its lease, which the AARP insists, to this day, be kept confidential—even from its own members—clearly reveals this. The 204-page document with twenty-four exhibits establishes beyond doubt AARP's primacy as an overseer with the legal right to make whatever design changes it chose.

But the lease isn't the only hard proof that AARP didn't just stumble across some space for rent. Further proof comes from the Washington architect responsible for the working drawings, Vlastimil Koubek. Koubek recalls that the drawings took him eight months, during which time he worked closely with AARP officials, including Horace Deets.[3] Needless to say, Koubek was well paid for his attentiveness to AARP's needs and whims. He couldn't remember what the fee was, but 4 percent to 7 percent of the construction cost is standard. At an estimated total construction cost of $130 million, that meant Koubek and associates snagged a cool $5 million, minimum. If AARP was looking for a good deal, it could have moved just a few miles south from their former K Street location into Virginia, where real estate is substantially cheaper. But of course price wasn't the top priority, moving closer to Capitol Hill to lobby Congress was.

Some who got early peeks at the E Street building disapproved of the expensive move. Sensing possible discord, the AARP leadership produced a fourteen-page glossy brochure entitled *Your Move*. These words appear under the subheading, "Why we're moving":

> Our commitment to quality service to members is unwavering. Providing top-notch service requires top-notch effort, efficiency, and equipment. Our decision to relocate and move our Washington, D.C. staff under one roof is crucial to fulfilling our on-going pledge to provide the best service possible now....

NONSENSE, ONE SENIOR AARP official told me: "We are supposed to be a *service* organization, not a serve-yourself one. We needed to be under one roof, but it didn't have to be a gold one."

AARP downplayed the move. In the monthly *AARP Bulletin*, it was buried on Page 17, as one of several items in the "Bulletin Board" section, with a small picture. It was three paragraphs:

> A handsome new building—accessible to wheelchairs and designed with the needs of staff, volunteers, members, and visitors in mind—now houses AARP's one thousand–plus Washington employees.

> The move consolidates operations formerly spread throughout six locations in the nation's capital. The new building includes a video production studio, visitor center, and staff cafeteria.

> In addition to its Washington headquarters, AARP has ten regional and two state offices across the country.

THE ONLY WAY the embarrassing move could have been more understated would have been no mention at all.

"When I first came here after the old building, I was embarrassed," said one African American secretary. "But I got used to it. I mean, I work overtime and don't get paid for it." A well-paid computer programmer said she thought it was too plush, for a few days anyway. "But then I was just so impressed with myself when I got my own office."

While staffers appreciated the luxury, they also worried about the message it sent. One particularly searing indictment came from an anonymous female staffer ("Miss X") in a highly confidential, late 1994 "diversity study." The AARP wouldn't release the unsanitized version to its own staffers. My copy is stamped "CONFIDENTIAL." Consider some remarks:

The Building: The ostentation of the building itself sets off visiting members. One greeter assigned to deal with "walk-ins" (members arriving without appointments) recounted frequent disapproving remarks: "I've had visitors come to me and say, 'This is horrible!' And the stock answer I was instructed to give was, 'We do not own the building. We only lease the building.' Of course, this just means we waste more money since a decade of paying the rent covers the full cost of the building in the first place. The one member I remember best shook her head, looking around her, and quoted the Bible: 'Vanity of vanities, this is vanity.'"

The Furniture: The ergonomically correct chairs came at $300 a pop. The AARP is now locked into a one-design furniture mentality that requires staffers to order the same expensive bookcases, desks, chairs, and such as needed. The association is forever having to defend itself against the charge, made in an earlier *Washington Monthly* article, that "in 1990, AARP spent more than twice as much money on furniture for its posh headquarters ($29 million) as it spent on programs assisting the elderly ($14 million)." The AARP explains that this represented a one-time investment in quality furniture that will last for years, but, alas, in vain. Visiting member complaints about the accoutrements are second only to those about the building itself.

The Artwork: [In *AARP World* documents, it's all one word.] These are the wall-hangings and such that were bought to please the members. They haven't. The more vociferous tell them they should have saved the members' money. Special nicknames have been given to several of the artworks. And the Virginia art of "We Two" in one of the lobbies, which looks sort of like large, acrylic-on-wood paper doll cutouts of a girl and a boy, has been decorated with sombreros, bikinis, and other assortment of clothing.

The Doors: The building complies with the American Disabilities Act requirements, exceeding them in some cases. But the entrance doors are a problem. When the automatic doors break down, visitors must use the massive bronze-casted steel doors that are far too heavy for the frailer elderly to open. Miss X in her survey remarked: "The doors are heavier than ten-ton bricks. We are an association for retired persons, so most of your clients coming in this door are going to be fifty, sixty, and up. You have one handicap door that sometimes does not work, but then the other door takes (even) me a good pull to get it open."

The Marble Floors: This organization has issued a separate "Product Report" advisory on what to look for in canes and walking sticks, and should be familiar with their use. But they forgot all about it when it came to the Italian marble floors. Again, Madame X says it best: "The marble floors are slippery and are hard for elderly people with canes. I love the marble floors. They're beautiful, but they're not practical."

The Temperature Controls: Overall, the building's super-duper controls are set not for the elderly but for the young. The elderly tend to feel the cold more, so a shivering, sweater-wearing older employee is not an uncommon sight at 601 E Street. An unprepared visiting member doesn't stand a chance.

The Awnings: Primarily decorative, the awnings offer no respite to pedestrians. Conversation in the rooftop Operations Center: *Engineer:* "We also control our awnings with this computer. When it's raining, the awnings come in. When it's blowing too hard, the awnings come in. If it was a sunny day today, with no wind, they'd be out. They're not out today: it's raining, and it's windy." *Author:* "Don't you want to cover people when they're walking?" *Engineer:* "These are fabric awnings! Are you kidding me? You know what they'd look like after they'd been rained on a couple of times and rolled up? They'd look like an old moldy rug that you'd find in a garage!"

In 1990, the AARP spent more than twice as much money on furniture for its posh headquarters as it spent on programs assisting the elderly.

The Security: This intimidates some visiting members, but the staff is grateful because security was a serious concern particularly to female staffers at 1909 K Street. "We had a lot of strange homeless people near the building there," says one. "It was just a safety concern. In the new building, I like the feeling." As for the homeless, old or young, "We keep them moving along," states the security chief.

The Soft Lighting: The truth is, AARP headquarters is friendlier to the blind than to those with aging sight; at least the blind have learned to walk in the dark. Paradoxically, the AARP hammers on hotels, corporations, and others that cater to the elderly to make sure rooms are well lit with 100- or greater watt light bulbs. But in its own headquarters, recessed lighting and dozens of 18-watt bulbs are the order of the day. A staffer in Member Services familiar with the problem adds: "If you're looking for a bright spot at headquarters, you're not going to find one. Everything is grey and blue, calm and soothing—and DARK! Older people can't see in the dim light. But you get off the elevator and it's so f——— dark you can't find your way to your own office. This is especially true in the wintertime, when it's dark outside. So many members have stumbled—and some have fallen—coming out of the elevator from the disorientation of it all."

Locked Bathrooms: Finally, there is the most humiliating indignity of all to which the AARP's current callous policy subjects its older members: locked bathrooms. The AARP has frequently educated others about two characteristics of some older individuals—a shyness in asking for help, and a problem with incontinence. What does this mean for the frail visitor to AARP headquarters? Madame X is particularly eloquent on this score: "A lot of members come in and need the bathroom doors permanently unlocked. There have been incidents where the member couldn't get in fast enough and urinated on him- or herself...."

ONE COULD CHARGE AARP'S leadership with rank hypocrisy, with *using* rather than *serving* its elderly members.

Chapter 4

Horace Who?

He may be the most powerful man in the United States outside government.

—*E.J. Kahn, Jr., The New Yorker*[1]

Other staffers kept coming up to me: they heard that I had spoken to Mr. Deets. The thing that I had done amazed them. Is it true? they asked. Kind of like I had a papal audience; it was that kind of awe.

—Mid-level AARP staffer, recounting the reaction of colleagues to a personal conversation with the executive director[2]

Horace Deets has a genial, warm smile over a chin dimple, friendly and understanding eyes behind unobtrusive thin-lensed glasses, and well-coiffed light brown hair—he could be popcorn king Orville Redenbacher's favorite brother. But don't be fooled by the folksy exterior. He is, in the boldface headline of a 1997 *Fortune* magazine profile: **Washington's Second Most Powerful Man.**[3]

Even so, Executive Director Horace Deets is also a genuine Washington mystery. Though he has headed the most powerful lobby in the world for a decade, few politicians would recognize him if he walked by in the halls. It is an anonymity he carefully cultivates, and perhaps even hides behind, like the wizard in the Emerald City. Even to his own staff, Deets is notoriously hard to get to know. His inscrutability is a plus because it means nobody can pin him down; he can keep moving. A gifted mimic at the AARP could never get Deets right. "It was like trying to impersonate a loaf of bread," she explained. "He's almost not a real person; he's two-dimensional."

The *Boston Globe* called him a "mild-mannered former South Carolina teacher"[4]; *Investor's Business Daily* saw him as "a quiet, self-deprecating man with a South Carolina drawl"[5]; *Regardie's* magazine said he was "no fireball."[6] So to say he is mellow is not revelatory. It is to say, instead, that he has a beatific, sometimes stultifying effect on others nearby. The sound of his voice can be massaging, in fact, his words a harmonic convergence of New Age bromides and homilies that reassure and soothe.

Not the kind of package one would expect to be able to steer AARP through the treacherous waters of the last decade, and what lies ahead. Behind him, he was responsible for AARP's two most serious lobbying debacles: the repeal of AARP-supported Medicare catastrophic coverage, and endorsement of Democratic health care reform bills. In front of him is an uncertain future with the transformation of AARP's constituency (those 50+) into a baby boomer contingent that may choose to boycott preferred AARP membership, or oppose it noisily. Whatever way he turns, *Fortune* predicted, "(his) obscurity can't last.... Deets can't remain faceless. His association is ground zero in what is shaping up as the first battle of the new millennium, a war not between countries or companies but between generations."

HORACE BELL DEETS, born in 1938, was raised in a middle class family in an old section of Charleston, South Carolina, known as Ashley Forest. He was the eldest of four children. His father was a civilian worker at the naval shipyards who began as apprentice and worked his way to retirement as superintendent of Shop #67, the key electronics shop at the yards. Horace was "a perfectly normal boy," recalls Horace's mother, Kitty.[7] "He climbed trees, built a treehouse with his friends."

Though the subject would later consume Horace's adult life, politics was rarely discussed in his childhood home, but religion was. Horace's father, a Methodist, had promised the Catholic priest who married them that he would raise the children in Kitty's faith, Catholicism. He was better than his word. The senior Deets, while being an active Methodist, made sure the rest of his family got to the Catholic church, since mother Kitty didn't drive. He helped build classrooms in that church and became so familiar with the local priest that "word was when Father McCarthy wanted to go to confession, he called Dad," says Horace's younger brother, John.[8] "Nothing ever left Dad. You could tell him anything in the world, and it remained with him."

> **Horace Deets has an uncertain future with the transformation of AARP's constituency into a baby boomer contingent that may choose to boycott preferred AARP membership, or oppose it noisily.**

Deets attended the premier Catholic high school of the area, Bishop England High School. Named for the first bishop of Charleston, it boasted a near-100 percent acceptance rate for college among its graduates. Horace, nicknamed "Deetsy" by chums, became president of the French Club, and served with the Key Club.[9] Clean-cut and quiet, he wasn't big on sports, didn't date much or get into trouble. Younger brother John joked that while he learned "first hand" (pun intended) that nuns and priests could discipline rather smartly, this never happened to Horace. "It wasn't that he was an obedient puppy, because he was his own person. He was just never in a position where he compromised himself; he followed the rules."

Deets was studious, achieving an A– average, graduating twelfth out of eighty-one students. The Class of '56 high school annual— called *The Miscellany* after the first Catholic newspaper in the United States, which had been started by Bishop John England— reported that Deetsy, a boy who "never makes an enemy," was headed for the Coast Guard Academy. His brother said that Horace was rejected for being underweight, so he steered in another direction, the priesthood.

Going to St. Bernard's, a small four-year seminary college in

Alabama run by the Benedictine order, was a serious undertaking. Others dropped out after the first or second year, like brother John Deets and Horace's first roommate, high school senior class president John Lavelle. Lavelle found St. Bernard's more constricting than the well-disciplined Deets.[10] "Imagine going from high school, where I used to go out every night and date, and played football, and then making this complete 360-degree change where you get up at 4:30 or 5 o'clock in the morning, and do meditation, and go to mass, sing Gregorian chants, study all day, sing psalms at night, and have vespers and so on. Well, you *have* to have a sense of humor to survive." In fact, he says, Deets did. Consigned to a basement at first because they were underclassman, Lavelle laughed at recalling how they dispatched the field mice overrunning their quarters. He would play a requiem while Deets, in all solemnity, dropped the mice in the toilet and, to the flushing, pronounced part of last rites, "In nomine patris, et filii et spiritus sancti.…"

Deets received a bachelor's degree from St. Bernard's in 1960, having specialized in philosophy and history. He concentrated on theology and education while attending Catholic University in Washington, D.C., for the next four years. His intention had always been to return as a parish priest to his home diocese of Charleston, possibly as a teacher as well. According to *The Official Catholic Directory*, Father Deets was ordained as a Diocesan priest at least by 1966 and disappeared from the rolls of active priests after 1973. Horace's mother recalled he was a priest for twelve years before "retiring."

According to Deets's own account, he served the bishop of Charleston in a variety of capacities, including as a parish priest, giving communion, hearing confession, and so on.[11] He was a Diocesan priest, meaning he belonged to no separate order like the Jesuits or Franciscans. "I would do whatever assignments were given to me by the Bishop [of the Diocese] within the state of South Carolina. Sometimes it was parish work; sometimes it was school work; sometimes it was administrative work. It just depended." He taught a variety of courses—algebra, English, Latin, history—and took up school administrative duties for several years at Bishop England and other locations.

In the early 1970s, for unexplained reasons, Father Deets decided to leave the pastoral and teaching world. He moved to the Washington, D.C., area and began work for the Equal Employment Opportunity Commission, designing and delivering training programs for their personnel. His next stint was as Director of Outreach at the Washington Hospital Center, where he developed programs to combat alcohol and drug abuse in the workplace. Deets had also

Deets's salary and benefits in 1995 totaled $357,201—not counting the perks.

come to the attention of AARP's Executive Director Harriet Miller by the mid-1970s. She was so enchanted with Deets that she first hired him as a consultant writing grants for AARP in July 1975.

It was a time when the AARP hierarchy in Washington seemed to have an affinity for ex-Catholic priests and nuns. "We used to hire them all the time," recalled one former senior staffer. "These were people who decided they didn't want to be celibate or religious anymore, still wanted to do some good and this place fit their sensibilities. But they were not very high-achieving people. They certainly weren't the kind of movers and shakers that could get a bill through Congress."

Still, as late as the 1990s, non–Catholic AARP staffers complained about a profusion of Catholic "ex-es" in key positions. In 1994, for instance, Deets the ex-priest was the top staffer as executive director, his chief of staff was an ex-priest, there were two other ex-priests and one ex-nun working for the Office of the Executive Director, and the head of the Human Resources Department (personnel) was an ex-nun.

Though obviously unintended, Horace Deets made his career at AARP stepping over the bodies of ousted personnel.

When an AARP personnel director was fired in the fall of 1975, Deets stepped easily into the position. In 1978 he moved up to work for new Executive Director Cy Brickfield, first as his gofer and then as his chief of staff. In 1984 the director of Legislation—the lobbying arm—was fired and Deets was drafted as acting director for eight months. He moved from there in 1985 to be acting director of public relations, and then back to chief of staff for Brickfield, a role

Deets continued faithfully through Brickfield's successor, Executive Director Jack Carlson. The explosive January 1988 firing of Carlson, AARP's one and only Republican executive director, shifted Deets into position as the acting director.

When the board settled on Horace Deets as the permanent executive director in mid-March he was only forty-nine, too young even to join the AARP. A former top AARP employee called it a classic case of "slow and steady wins the race. The tortoise Horace won." But the selection of Deets was described by another staffer as a "*huge* surprise. He may have punched all those tickets, but he didn't have the background for his position. Here he was, jumping from chief of staff to executive director. But the board just looked at him, I guess, and said, he appears to be doing things we like, not causing any waves, so we'll just let Horace do it. Then voila! He triples his salary overnight."

Deets's salary as the head of a do-gooder organization rankles rank-and-file AARP members when they learn of it. His salary and benefits in 1995 totaled $357,201—not counting the perks.[12] And this is a *nonprofit* organization, a service organization. (In way of contrast, Elizabeth Dole earned much less, about $200,000, heading up the American Red Cross, which is three times the size financially as AARP.) An even more salient comparison is to realize that in 1995 alone *the membership dues of at least 70,000 members were swallowed up for Deets's salary and benefits.*

THERE IS ONE THING that Horace Deets can't seem to tolerate—or at least tolerate a discussion about: his priestly past.

Handwritten notes from the late Jack Carlson, Deets's predecessor as executive director, reveal: "Deets sensitive about perception as Parish Priest—told him I thought it showed someone concerned about people—psychology and sociology."

Months later, after Carlson was fired, Deets had AARP's public relations people carefully *rephrase* the priestly part of his life. "He was a teacher and a school administrator in South Carolina for eight years," the first AARP press release read,[13] announcing his assumption as acting executive director. The profile on him in the *AARP News Bulletin*, March 1988, also noted only that he had been "a teacher and school administrator in South Carolina." The follow-up official AARP press release repeated the phrase "teacher and school administrator in South Carolina for eight years." Certainly it is no idle oversight to fail to mention he was an ordained priest in the Catholic Church.

That this is not a niggling matter but a key to his character is evident from conversations with friends and AARP colleagues who aver it is a subject he continues to avoid. "You just knew not to press it, why he went into the priesthood, and why he left," said one. Another friend said that, over the years, Deets was the only ex-priest at AARP who "took umbrage" being asked about that part of his life. But then, he continued, Horace was a man so private that for years he did not speak much about his wife or family. "I thought that [his having been a priest] was probably something that was personal enough in his life that I did not probe it," Board Chairman Robert Shreve said.

Perhaps it has something to do with the fact that he didn't just "retire" and go off quietly into the sweet post-priestly goodnight. He forsook his vow of celibacy, married a divorcée, and began attending the Episcopalian Church. Despite all that, as one Catholic AARP associate noted, "since he was ordained a priest, he can still function as one. He can still say mass. He can be released from his vows, but his priesthood is irrevocable and forever, according to the rite of Melchizedek."

It was Horace Deets, however, who ended a decades-old, successful inter-faith program that his predecessors found valuable, and that obviously served the aims of AARP Founder Ethel Percy Andrus, who placed a premium on religious values.

The AARP's inter-religious programs were formalized after the 1971 White House Conference on Aging. "The spiritual needs of the aging really are those of every person, writ large: the need for identity, meaning, love and wisdom,"[14] the Conference determined. Delegates called on religious communities to respond to help older persons remain creative and caring as long as possible.

A year later, AARP Executive Director Bernard Nash authorized $3,000 to help launch the National Interfaith Coalition on Aging (NICA). In 1974 he hired The Rev. Earl Kragnes as a full-time coordinator for the AARP's own interfaith efforts, often done in coordination with NICA.

Conferences were held, and useful pamphlets—such as a 1993 AARP publication, *The Clergy: Gatekeepers for the Future*—were distributed to help pastors understand the spiritual and physical needs of aging parishioners.

But Deets ordered Kragnes to phase out the program and its volunteers. Kragnes later concluded that the association's leaders, beginning with Deets, were uncomfortable dealing with the spiritual aspect of the elderly. "I felt that there was a kind of suspicion, and *maybe an antipathy*, on the part of the AARP leadership about relating to the religious field, even getting into that. The staff would look at me, like, What are you doing this for?"[15]

Deets's discomfort with religion in part explains the sad story of Robert Covais. At fifty-eight, he was informed that the AARP travel office in which he was working would be shut down. He was promised preferential treatment for other AARP jobs that opened up; he had AARP awards, performance reviews, and recommendations to verify he was a valued employee. He accepted management's assurance at face value, and dutifully applied for post after post. But nothing happened.

A year and a half later—still unemployed, suffering from chronic back pain, and lacking AARP's health insurance—Covais learned the truth: he had unwittingly committed the unpardonable sin of appealing directly to Horace Deets for assistance. He had overstepped his boundaries. Never mind that this was the very thing that Deets, in his pastoral role as kind uncle of the staff, had encouraged. Trouble was, Covais believed him.

Covais, it turned out, had sent Deets a letter describing his difficulties in late 1994. The following April, he finally received a cold three-paragraph memo from Deets instructing him to work with the "appropriate people in HRD [Human Resources

Department]."[16] Translation: Don't bother me. It was precisely the kind of cruel brush-off that AARP decries when other companies shunt aside *their* older workers during downsizing periods. Deets put out the word that he didn't want Covais around the association.

But it may not have been Robert's letter that unsettled Deets. Deets had received a private Christmastime letter at his home from Robert's pastor, Father James Healy. Father Healy, an outspoken advocate of social justice and human rights issues, was exactly the kind of activist AARP and its executive director extolled.

> There is one thing that Horace Deets can't seem to tolerate: his priestly past.

Healy wrote to Deets that Robert had come to him "in great distress" over pending unemployment.[17] He was seeking Deets's "gracious cooperation in clarifying the facts and issues." Robert was particularly concerned about the loss of health insurance, Healy informed Deets, because he "was put on short-term disability earlier this year for degenerative spinal disc disease for which he underwent almost six months of treatment." He followed with some pointed questions, intended to stir Deets's conscience. "Is it possible that [AARP] wants to put this 'older' employee out to pasture and replace him in a year or so with younger, less expensive staff? Is it possible that, on the one hand, AARP promotes the values of older employees, and on the other hand, terminates them with no concern for either ability to find work elsewhere, or without concern for health issues? Was the cost of health care for this person a factor in determining that he would not be offered the same job protection as the minority woman in her 30s?"

Deets seethed. He viewed it as an insufferable invasion of privacy. At least that's how it was described during a closed-door personnel appeals board hearing of Covais's case in the summer of 1996. Among the key findings of the board,[18] which included both management and staff representation, was that Covais had been promised at least one "viable job offer" within six months of his termination, but it had never materialized. "The Human Resources Staff member assigned to help the grievant did not provide any significant assistance," the board found. But the key management representative at the hearing, according to the board memo, concluded that Covais had significantly damaged his own cause through "inappropriate conduct, including the sending of letters to the executive director's home." In the actual hearing, the senior AARP official was even more frank about the effect of the priest's sympathetic appeal to Deets: "*No hiring manager at AARP would dare place someone who pissed off the executive director!*"

HORACE DEETS HAS TO PLEASE only one group of people... the AARP Board of Directors—and not even all of them.

Since a six-member executive committee of the board is the only group with the power to fire him, Horace has been careful to cultivate their glowing view of him. Robert Shreve, the departing chairman of the board in 1996, told me that there is no behind-the-scenes board effort to oust Deets, as there had been for several of his predecessors. He is not blamed for AARP's leadership failures.

A confidant of Deets's said, "A smart executive director should be spending 80 percent of his time with the board—Horace knows. At the board meetings, if you see the board looking to the attorney more than they look to you, you're in deep trouble. Horace has worked with the board very well—kept them dependent on him, and his advice."

Still, the future is not clear sailing for Deets. For example, he recently tried to strip the board of staff support they rely on for assessments and information independent of the executive director. The board revolted, and Deets backed off.

There is the two-year reign of Helen Boosalis as chairman of the board, which began in 1996. Boosalis is the former Democratic mayor of Lincoln, Nebraska. Though she doesn't know it, Horace has privately expressed a serious distaste of her to at least one friend. "She's very outspoken, which has irritated Horace, the friend said. "'She asks too many questions,' he complained to me more than once." Bad blood with such a potentially powerful board member is poor strategy.

Moreover, Horace Deets knows better than anyone else at AARP that being executive director is not an appointment for life. "I like to point this out to people," he says. "I worked for four executive directors of AARP, only one of whom left voluntarily."[19]

Perhaps this fear of being toppled, as his unfortunate predecessors were, helps explain his fascination with trendy management theories. Deets, like many who have left a religious commitment, goes in for the "sharing" and "caring" school of management, and offers a panoply of classes and seminars to staff. The AARP invests more than $2 million a year training staff in courses like "Presentation Skills," "Behavioral Interviewing," "Writing for the Information Age," "Grant Writing and Grant Seeking," and so on. A large percentage of AARP employees take advantage of these courses, which inevitably drains the time they spend on their salaried jobs. An anonymous AARP manager, replying to a 1995 survey, wrote: "Wish you could limit the number of hours they can take a year [for training programs]."

Lower staffers have also picked up the idea that Deets vacillates on management theory, based on the latest book he's read. Acronyms like CQI (Continuous Quality Improvement) and ACE (Align, Create, and Empower) have become shopworn to subordinates. Asked in an employee survey why they thought the association was initiating a new goal, one replied: "The executive director read a book; it's the latest in organizational theory."

In April 1995 Horace eagerly passed out copies of Betsy Sanders's *Fabled Service: Ordinary Acts, Extraordinary Incomes* to senior staff. "Fabulous service," he said, quoting the book, "is quite simply ordinary people doing ordinary things extraordinarily well."[20] One senior staffer noted sourly: "See, Horace keeps forgetting his Ecclesiastes, that there's 'nothing new under the sun.' He hires all these management consultants, and it's just money thrown out. He buys one fad after another, whether it's Drucker, Peters, Bennis or whoever. A consultant comes up with a great new concept which is probably fifty years old with a different name, and Horace buys it. He's got consultants running around all the time doing this crap."

Another example of a Deetsism is a high-tech "Decision Support System" he was enthused about using. He ordered the appropriate programming, and made it available to all senior managers. The system was accessible for almost two years before it was abandoned, at a cost of at least $100,000. An internal auditor required to take a close look at the expenditure focused on a single nine-month period and discovered that the only person who had ever logged onto the system was Deets himself, and he'd done it only once.

When the new building was erected, another Deets enthusiasm was fulfilled. His dream of a first-class training center came true. The training center idea was backed by one of those task forces he so loves. The dream added at least $1 million to the cost of the building.[21]

Renamed the AARP Learning Center, it is where hundreds of AARP staffers wile away thousands of hours taking courses related— and not so related—to their jobs. Lower staff are allowed to take only those courses their managers approve; upper staff can feast and frolic in the "warm space" at their pleasure. "There is a certain amount of favoritism and cronyism to it all," says one AARP staffer.

What goes on at these training sessions? People unleash their creativity and learn about teamwork. And they play games. In one especially memorable session/game the class entered the Learning Center—now looking much like a kindergarten. Class members were encouraged to create something out of the Elmer's glue, ribbons, sticks, bows, crayons, sparklers, stars, and colored paper, among other things, on the tables. The class leader then "challenged" everyone, "I want everybody to take their creativity back to their office. Whenever you're in the doldrums, feeling uninspired, I want you to look at this thing and realize it means, I'm creative."

So far no one has stifled Horace Deets's creativity when it comes to spending money.

Chapter 5

Far from the Founder

My opinion is that AARP is a suspicious organization
and I would like to know who started it and is
behind it.

—Hazel Eckburg, Princeton, Illinois[1]

I joined the AARP because it *was* a noble idea....

*—Gerald L. Guthrie, former
AARP member, Sherman, Texas*[2]

Ethel Percy Andrus was one of the truly great women of recent
American history; an unveering crusader for the dignity of the
elderly. So remarkable was she that inevitably Andrus was compared, in her day, to Clara Barton and Juliette Low, founders of the
Red Cross and Girl Scouts, respectively. "These visionary women
created these three big national institutions; they could see what was
needed,"[3] said one former senior AARP official. William Fitch,
AARP's first executive director, gave Andrus and Israeli Prime
Minister Golda Meir equal esteem "as two great pioneering
women."[4] Fitch should know. He worked for both of them.

Another former senior AARP official who worked closely with Andrus, Ernest Giddings, was more eloquent: "If you asked me what were the greatest personal qualities of Dr. Andrus, I would say, number one, her ability to inspire others. Second, her vision to see ahead, far, far into the future. Third, her philosophy of helping others.... Dr. Andrus inspired us to help others all the days of their lives."[5]

"TO TELL THE STORY of one's life, I imagine one begins with one's birth," Ethel Andrus began disarmingly in an unfinished autobiography.[6] "Mine took place in San Francisco, on September 21, 1884. My parents were young folk, eager, dedicated and very, very human. My father, George Wallace Andrus, was a struggling young attorney... and my mother [Lucretia Duke] his proud and admiring helpmate," the daughter of a British sea captain who remained in California after docking there on the day that gold was discovered.

Over the mantel of the dining room of Ethel's childhood home, engraved on a plank of manzanita wood, were these words:

> Three pleasant things—
> To be here
> To be here together and
> To think well of one another.

It was a sweet sentiment that summed up Andrus's genial opinion of the human race. She once wrote of her favored generation, "We have lived in a time of cozy homes and hearthsides. No matter how urban they might have seemed to us, there was still a bit of earth about where a father was revered as lawmaker, as priest, as judge, and loved as father. And mother was adored as she soothed and comforted us. There were chores about and obligations to which we were held, and perhaps a family sing and family prayers. We know that we were the fortunate ones. We had a job to do and we were expected to do it. We were expected to be present and attentive and not to participate, but always to be loved."

It was an idyllic childhood she and her only sibling (older sister Maud) enjoyed, as Ethel described it to friends. There was the wait at San Juan Capistrano for the swallows to return on St. Joseph's Day, the traveling marionette Punch and Judy shows, Friday afternoon recitals, fascination with the hurdy-gurdy man and the monkey in his red jacket and white-feathered green cap, and the hunts for four-leaf clovers amid the sweet scents of geranium, heliotrope, and jasmine.

A charter member of the AARP saw the nonpartisan association transformed from a senior's organization into a liberal, big-government lobbying organization.

And looming above it all, authoritatively but kindly, was her father, whose preachments revolved around two constellations—work and service. She took this to heart, as much from a daughter's love as observation. Little Ethel would sometimes risk being late to school just to watch a farrier shoeing a horse. "It was a thrilling sight: he was so absorbed, so at one with the animal whose shoe he was fitting, so dexterous with his bellows and his fire, sometimes smoldering and smoky and sometimes shooting up in brilliant flames. With glowing iron in hand, his shop so redolent always of that pungent acrid smell of burned hoof, he would say at just the last moment, 'Scurry along, Sissie, or you'll be late!' Scurrying away, I would feel the call of service, of joy in work, of being meaningful. Even today as I write I am thinking as I did then that one of nature's masterpieces is a man absorbed in his work and loving it."[7]

An early hero of hers was Peter Cooper, an inventor and innovator in American steelmaking and other industries, who was a generous philanthropist like his contemporary Andrew Carnegie. Once again, his civic service was what moved Ethel Andrus. Her father had said, "We must give of ourselves to our fellows, must do some good, somewhere, for which we would receive no pay other than satisfaction of the doing." Not unexpectedly, after the family moved to Chicago and she began a career as a teacher, Ethel spent all her spare time serving at two settlement houses—Chicago Commons, and the more famous Hull House run by social reformer Jane Addams.

One contemporary of Andrus, gerontologist Dr. James A. Peterson, who also worked in a Chicago settlement house, said such an experience was pivotal in Andrus's evolution. "Working in a settlement house in Chicago in those days was very eye-opening and gave you a certain sophistication because we were dealing with all the immigrant groups who were coming in. We were dealing with utter poverty—90 percent of the people in my area were unemployed and on relief, although there wasn't any relief. That was so tragic. So that I'm sure she picked up some of her social concern from Jane Addams." Not only that, but Addams's progressive work in the women's suffrage movement must have also rubbed off on Andrus. "Jane Addams had that philosophy that, 'We *can* do,' and she *did*. And Ethel Percy Andrus, nothing daunted her. Throughout her whole life there was nothing that interfered. She set a goal; she achieved it."

In 1910 she returned with her family to California, a move prompted by her father's failing health. In 1916 Andrus became the first female high school principal in California. Under her leadership, Abraham Lincoln High School gained national recognition.

She explained there was no secret to her success. It was simply "to bring to each a sense of his own worth by treating him with dignity and respect...."

She gave students unprecedented responsibility in running the school. "Somehow you found yourself acting the way she wanted you to," a once-wayward student later recalled.

One boy who was elected president of the student council arrived for his swearing-in wearing clothes that Andrus thought were too casual. "Don't you have a suit?" she asked.

"No, this is all I have," came the reply.

"You're wrong, you have a suit," said the principal, as she pressed some money into the boy's hand. He returned in a suit, and proudly presided over his first student council.

After voluntarily retiring at sixty-five to care for her ailing mother, Andrus signed on as welfare director for the California Retired Teachers Association, and soon became appalled at the poverty of teachers living on small state pensions. One day, a friend handed Andrus a dollar bill and said, "Here are my dues for a national organization" to help retired teachers. More dollar bills arrived as retired teachers spread the word about Andrus's ambition to help them. Eventually, Andrus founded the National Retired Teachers Association (NRTA), whose members later became the nucleus of the AARP.

Andrus's motto was "To serve and not be served." What AARP's lobbyists are doing today is exactly the reverse of what she envisioned.

The formal beginning of the AARP came in a meeting of the NRTA at the Woodner Hotel in Washington, D.C., on April 30, 1958. "The meeting was called to order for the purpose of creating a sister organization allied and parallel to NRTA but independent of it."[8] It was noted that so many nonteachers were trying to link themselves to the NRTA to join its health insurance plan and enjoy other benefits that it was time to create a general association for all American retired people. On July 1 the AARP was officially incorporated in Washington, D.C.

To get the word out about the new AARP, Andrus created its publication *Modern Maturity* for an annual membership fee of $2. Andrus put in sixteen-hour days. The staff followed Andrus's work ethic by coming in on Saturdays and working overtime without extra compensation. Andrus herself never received a salary, only expenses—and was decidedly unimpressed with money, big or small.

Dr. Andrus oversaw everything from strategic planning to paper clips, including the daily details of staffing, hiring, salaries, and other financial aspects of the fast-growing organization.

Andrus could be a demanding boss, demanding the best that the staff could offer—but no more. She knew not all her associates could be as accomplished as she was in so many fields. "We need not be as versatile as Thomas Jefferson," she once said, "about whom it was told that he could calculate an eclipse, survey an estate, argue a cause, break a horse, dance a minuet and play the violin."[9] Together, combining all their talents, her vision of AARP would reach fruition. And though she accepted good suggestions, her word was final.

Contemporaries of hers agreed that Andrus shone most when speaking. But the only way to make an organization grow quickly, she knew, was not speech by speech, but by getting the national spotlight. She proved masterful at getting such publicity. The four key events that propelled AARP membership during the Andrus years were her Congressional testimony before an antitrust commission, her prominent participation in the first White House Conference on Aging, a favorable article in *Reader's Digest,* and an AARP exhibit at the New York World's Fair. She continued to work until killed by a massive heart attack two months short of her 83rd birthday. Even then, she wrote until her last hours in a Los Angeles hospital.

In the wake of her death, many memorials took place, including one in Washington, D.C., arranged by her friend, future Secretary of Defense Melvin Laird. But while many paid their respects to her memory and to her work with the AARP, the association began changing in unwelcome ways. Ruth Lana, Andrus's friend and a charter member of the AARP, saw the nonpartisan association transformed from a senior's organization into a liberal, big-government lobbying organization. In an interview shortly before her own death, she said, "Ethel believed... there was a place for the government to stop. Now, maybe I shouldn't be saying that but that was the impression that I had. She felt if the government took over the responsibility of the people, the people wouldn't have any incentive. And she felt everybody should have an incentive, something to work for and to work. She was a Republican, but [no one] ever knew it. She used to say, 'No one knows what my party affiliation is.' She did not believe that we should become a country dominated by the government. That was her philosophy. I don't know what she would have done [with AARP] today."[10]

Andrus had founded the AARP as a service organization, to take despairing retirees and help them find useful work. "If you picture life as a long arc beginning at birth and traversing the span of life towards death, we can see on the one end of that arc the babe, any babe, your beloved grandchild it might well be. To him, the world is himself, his comforts, the attention he craves.... At the other end of the arc is the Man of God, the Christ who gave his all—even his life, to the betterment of his fellows—to point the way to selfless service."

And that was to be the goal of the AARP. Andrus's motto was "To serve and not be served."

Reading the more than one hundred editorials Ethel Percy Andrus wrote, one sometimes feels one is listening to a speaker at a Republican convention:

> Today it often seems that our people—good, sturdy folk, too—are divided among those who believe that America owes them a living and who search ever for security and ease by minimizing the old economic virtues of prudence, thrift and sturdy and honorable independence, and the manlier ones of effort, adventure and freedom.[11]

The AARP has strayed far from the vision of its founder, Ethel Percy Andrus.... Today, the AARP equates dignity with the dollars it can dig out of the federal purse.

> Our founding fathers knew that the primary threat to the natural rights of man has always been government.... Always the fight for freedom has been waged by the people against their government.... Let us not forget that the Bill of Rights... is really a Bill of Prohibitions against our own government, stating specifically that the government must not destroy our rights.[12]

> The question now confronts us: How did it happen that so many have substituted, in their thinking, governmental dependence for self-faith and self-reliance, the need of security for a drive toward self-development, the protection of socialized benefits in place of the rewards for individual effort, the escape into anonymity instead of involvement in the unpleasant or the strange? Can we, without protest, without effort, stand by and see America sold so short?[13]

TODAY'S AARP STAFF LEADERS and lobbyists would do well to read the one editorial in which Andrus spelled out succinctly in two parallel columns "What AARP Is" and "What AARP Is Not."[14] In this, she emphasized [italics added]:

—We know that most older persons are able to live in independence and dignity. *AARP does not welcome the welfare state as the way of life for all older persons.*

—AARP is an organization of older folk who believe in keeping alive their interests, in broadening their horizons and maintaining an image of aging for themselves as one of growth and service. *It is not organized to seek government relief and direction.*

—AARP engages itself, with deep concern and conviction, in a practical fashion, to increase for its members the purchasing power of the retirement dollars *in direct contrast to seeking welfare subsidies and benefits from the Federal Government.*

"Those who lead AARP have always been able to look to the words of our founder, the late Dr. Ethel Percy Andrus, for guidance and inspiration,"[15] Horace Deets wrote in his first editorial after becoming AARP chief executive in 1988. "There's not anything we're doing that that lady didn't think of."[16] But what AARP's lobbyists are doing today is exactly the reverse of what she envisioned.

An address incoming AARP President Eugene Lehrmann gave to the 1994 Biennial Convention in Anaheim, California, highlights the turnabout: "We're here today because [of] Ethel Percy Andrus. [But] times have changed—and so must AARP's outlook."[17] A year later, Lehrmann led the board of directors in endorsing the Mitchell-Gephardt health care reform bill, which would have imposed government control over the entire health industry, at enormous cost to taxpayers. If Andrus were still alive, she would have been among the thousands of disgruntled AARP members jamming its phone lines after that endorsement.

Ethel Percy Andrus has been ill-served by the modern leaders of the organization she founded. She is now only an afterthought in speeches. She deserves better, though, as we will see, her judgment was not perfect.

Chapter 6

The Sweetheart Deal

> AARP and Leonard Davis played a shell game that was unbelievable. The guy lost his insurance license because he was untrustworthy. But he figured a way with AARP to get around the law by peddling insurance to a captive audience with volunteers doing the peddling. And it worked, big time. The whole root of AARP is a guy who was cutting corners.
>
> *—former Senator Alan Simpson*[1]

> Leonard Davis is a name that is not uttered within the four walls of AARP anymore.
>
> *—John Rother, director of AARP's Legislative Division*[2]

The AARP was founded on a Faustian bargain. Andrus wanted to establish a health insurance organization for retired teachers like herself. But insurance companies wouldn't sell health insurance to older people. Enter Leonard Davis.

Davis, one of New York's leading insurance brokers, had already experimented with health insurance policies for senior citizens. His first experience had come when the Atlantic City Electric Company insisted that any group health policy cover their retired employees. After doing the actuarial work, Davis became convinced that policies for older people could turn a neat profit. He realized that the ratio of healthy to sick elderly would actually be in his favor. This was a revolutionary insight which made Davis a rich man.

Davis got his second shot when Robert Decormier, a Poughkeepsie Democratic politico, asked him to develop a similar plan for New York's retired teachers.[3] Davis, intrigued, approached the Chicago-based Continental Casualty Company (later CNA Financial Corporation) with a plan. It cost $5 a month, and benefits were worked out with minute care. Continental agreed to a trial run of a year. What made the plan attractive to teachers, who signed up enthusiastically, was that no physical was required.

Decormier was so elated with the results that he told his friend Ethel Percy Andrus about it. Andrus had knocked on the doors of forty-two insurance companies, seeking similar coverage for elderly teachers, and had been summarily dismissed as a little old lady playing businessman. Andrus was seventy and Davis an ambitious thirty-year-old, when they met in 1955. They hit it off immediately, and Davis agreed to design a plan for her retired teachers.

Launched in 1956, the Davis health insurance policies were wildly successful. Even Davis seemed astounded by the response. "You remember how we were prepared to handle about 5,000 applications when we first announced the plan?" Davis enthused in a letter to Andrus.[4] "Who would have dared to forecast that just a year later, better than 15,000 would have joined?" He noted that so far there had been a total of 2,500 claims and that $300,000 had been paid out in benefits. By the end of the first year Davis and Continental were averaging $75,000 a month in premiums and paying out only about $25,000—a 200 percent markup for overhead and profit each month! Even though Davis and Continental were making a fortune, the teachers believed they were dealing with altruists who were doing retired seniors a great favor.

As word spread, older people responded in great numbers. Naturally enough, older people who weren't retired teachers wanted to get in on it, too. Adding icing to the cake, officials at the U.S. Department of Health, Education and Welfare, in a meeting with Andrus, proclaimed the Davis plan "a significant social achievement." "Thousands of letters began to pour in from people who weren't teachers," an AARP history recalls.[5] "They were asking to obtain the insurance, too."

When Andrus and Ruth Lana, who functioned as Andrus's right-hand woman, decided that the teachers' association should be transformed into a broader organization for elderly people, Davis smelled opportunity. In the deal of a lifetime, Davis kicked in $50,000 in capital to start the AARP. The first *Modern Maturity*, the flagship publication that was to break records of its own, rolled off the presses in 1958. Andrus's inaugural message to the AARP, on the first page of the first issue of *Modern Maturity*, was an "invitation to security"—namely, the insurance plan sold by Davis.

During the early years, Andrus and Davis were regarded as cofounders of AARP. But it didn't take long for Davis to gain the upper hand. Under Davis, the AARP became a giant hybrid institution—a cash cow and a lobbying organization that fought for big government programs antithetical to the Republican philosophy of Ethel Andrus—but primarily after her 1967 death.

Andrus must have been dismayed by Davis's aggressive business practices, but the partnership survived a 1965 scandal that cost Davis his New York State insurance license because of "untrustworthiness." In that episode New York Insurance Department officials believed that Davis had condoned bribery and kickbacks involving a dental insurance plan. Davis denied the charge but was forced to surrender all New York insurance licenses.[6] This, however, did not prevent Davis from continuing his work with the AARP. By then he had become the prime minister, while Andrus reigned as queen, a much admired titular head but hardly the driving force. Davis emerged as the paramount figure only after Andrus died in 1967.

By that time, he had developed the AARP's most valuable asset: the list. The membership roll had been built in a number of ways. Davis ordered his insurance agents to come up with at least a thousand names a week. He knew that every new member was a potential customer, whether for health insurance or other products he would develop. In addition, NRTA members were leaned on to join the AARP. Even more creatively, Davis sent people to the Library of Congress to pore over old college alumni books to find people the right age for Davis's insurance policies. "He watched the magazine like a hawk," recalled Ruth Lana, "and he watched the lists forever, too. He controlled the list."

The AARP was already taking shape: a highly effective business machine attached to a program of good works. A 1971 internal history of the AARP noted: "If the business company tried to become a social institution, or the social institution tried to become a business, they would both lose what they had to give to each other."

But it didn't look like that to everybody. Outsiders often viewed the AARP as a business, plain and simple. Critics saw it more as a front for selling insurance policies. "It's really not too wrong to say that up until the late 1970s, the AARP was really owned and operated by the insurance industry," said Patrick Burns, communications director of the labor-backed National Council of Senior Citizens, a rival of the AARP. "They were just seen as apologists for the insurance industry, and they still sometimes are."

Davis watched his profits carefully. Before Andrus died, he had begun making noises about Continental Casualty, the original group health insurance underwriter. Davis was upset that "greedy" Continental agents were approaching senior citizens and selling them policies that didn't come through the AARP or Davis. There was nothing illegal about this. Indeed, one could view it as the happy fruition of Andrus's dream of widespread availability of health insurance for older people. But for Davis, it was undesired competition for his captive audience. He moved quickly to establish better control of this lucrative market. First came a scare campaign. "Warning to AARP Members," trumpeted a headline in the May 1967 *AARP News Bulletin*. "AARP members should be on their guard. Insurance agents and salesmen are approaching our members implying they represent AARP because they are identified with Continental Casualty Company, underwriters for AARP-sponsored Health Insurance. We have said it before—we say it again: AARP employs no salesmen or agents, Continental's or any other company's."

But warnings were not enough for Davis. In 1963 he had set about to protect his turf by establishing a Philadelphia-based holding company, the Colonial Penn Group, to act as the sole vendor of AARP insurance. Four years later, at a meeting held at Washington's Mayflower Hotel and immediately after a memorial service for Ethel Percy Andrus, the news was presented to the board as a *fait accompli*. No debate. "I never knew who approved the change; nobody objected. They were satisfied and Leonard had justified it," recalled William Fitch, an early AARP executive director, whose frequent opposition was a source of intense annoyance to Davis.[7]

Outsiders often viewed the AARP as a business. Critics saw it as a front for selling insurance policies.

Not surprisingly, since Colonial Penn was his creation, Davis was willing for the first time to surrender the AARP's most valuable possession—the mailing list—for a small fee. At this point, Davis *was* the AARP. He had done a brilliant job of consolidating his power, turning the AARP membership into a captive market for his insurance and other products. And he held the key people in thrall. For example, Davis had secured Ruth Lana's loyalty by hiring her to work for Colonial Penn, where her salary was considerably larger than AARP had paid. Lana, for her part, viewed Davis and herself as keepers of the flame that Ethel Andrus had lighted.

Indeed Davis's ability to charm older women who were the foundation of the AARP's prosperity inspired an inside joke. Grace Hatfield, a Davis favorite, was a retired schoolteacher who wrote a regular feature, mostly devoted to the virtues of the AARP-backed insurance policies, in *Modern Maturity*. Hatfield's picture, which ran with her column, showed a bespectacled, seemingly befuddled old lady looking away from the camera. People teased that she was looking to Davis for her cue.

Davis's most important move was installing his personal lawyers as AARP's lawyers. Wisely, he had allowed Andrus to choose her own accountants and bookkeepers. But legal counsel was another matter. Davis wanted lawyers who would be obligated to him. AARP's first general counsel was Philip L. Handsman, a close friend of Davis's and his personal legal advisor. Not coincidentally, Handsman was also a stockholder in Colonial Penn.

When Handsman died in 1971, a new firm was formed to handle AARP business—Miller, Singer, Michaelson & Raives. The two key partners, Alfred Miller and Lloyd Singer, were the power players who acted for Leonard Davis throughout the 1970s. Singer's *curriculum vitae* suggested what might have been a serious conflict of interest at another association. He had, at various times, been president of Colonial Penn Life Insurance Company, president of the board and chief executive officer of the Colonial Penn Corporation, and chairman of the board of the Colonial Penn Group, the holding group for all of Davis's companies.

When Davis wasn't available, Singer or Miller frequently sat in on AARP board meetings. In short, Davis and the lawyers ran the AARP. Indeed Harriet Miller, an AARP executive director turned hostile critic, named the two partners as correspondents in a $4 million suit. She charged that Davis kept the supposedly nonprofit AARP under his thumb through this "interlocking lawyer" arrangement.[8]

Wherever AARP had an important office—in Washington, D.C., California, or New York—Singer-Miller had an adjacent office. Like Davis, the firm got rich through the AARP. Its bill to AARP was at least $1 million a year for more than a decade.

One ten-page bill suggests that the New York lawyers were excessively involved in day-to-day business.[9] The three-month bill from the Singer-Miller firm, totaling $285,376.50 for AARP, claimed its lawyers spent a total of 1,629 hours "counseling" AARP's leadership during one three-month period, which included advice on subjects as far-ranging as Electronic Data Processing ($3,800); AARP Chapters ($3,500); Communications and Public Relations ($3,400); Publications and Advertising ($19,200); Copyright and Trademark Matters ($2,900); Leases, Real Estate Matters, Contracts ($6,900); and Miscellaneous Other Matters ($19,000).

AFTER BRINGING IN HIS OWN lawyers and currying favor with key people on the inside, Davis knew that, given the way the AARP was set up, his only threat could come from the board. But Davis made sure they were never so inclined. He took pains to see that they were tutored in AARP positions, first by Colonial Penn employees and then by Davis lackeys at AARP. Davis brooked no opposition.

He also made sure the board chairman was his choice. A confidential memo, written in 1973 by W.L. Mitchell, a board member, showed just how easy it was for Davis and his proxies to dominate the election process for chairman. Almost apologetically, Mitchell wrote then-Executive Director Bernard Nash that he was worried that the procedure for electing the chairman of the board "could be easily prearranged." As instituted, there was an open session, at which Davis or an ally was present. One person was nominated, seconded, and won in an uncontested open vote. That was it.

"It would be very embarrassing for a board member to raise a question or to make a second nomination once a nomination has been made and seconded," Mitchell noted. "At least one alternative might be to have the board meet for this purpose in executive session, or possibly with you in attendance, and have each of the board members privately submit a nomination for chairman to be followed thereafter by a secret vote for one of the nominees. The person receiving the highest number of votes would then be declared the chairman and the process would be regarded as fairer and more democratic."[10]

Mitchell's suggestion was ignored. But three years later, AARP president Alice VanLandingham complained, much more publicly, that she had been "bamboozled" during her first board election by the Davis faction.[11] VanLandingham confided in a memo that she was unwittingly part of a "fixed frame-up, even before I was officially installed. You saw it happen! When I was approached to nominate [one individual], I expected others to be nominated, and we could vote.... Right here, I should have said, 'This is our organization meeting. Please, let's have at least two nominations and let's vote.' Yes, you are right. It was fixed...."

But VanLandingham was no match for Davis. He knew how to control the meetings. Eugene Thrift, an independent accountant for AARP and admirer of Davis, often saw him in action. "I'd be giving financial reports, and he [Davis] would ask all kinds of questions, and keep me on my toes.... He wanted to know about everything."[12]

When Davis wanted something, he dispatched a cadre of experts to argue his position. An awed board inevitably backed Davis's agenda. VanLandingham found the whole thing shocking. She wrote bitterly to 150 fellow AARP volunteer leaders in 1978: "My last two years have taught me much.... Not until I was president did I realize the in-house games being played by the controlling group. This controlling group, under the guise of keeping all actions legal, operates our association. They wine and dine the national officers and board members. When any one of them questions anything, they are individually taken out to lunch."

Control, however, involved considerably more than wining and dining. Dissident Harriet Miller explained the method: "The meetings of the... board... are heavily attended by the lawyers and Davis himself, who primarily dominate the proceedings. Agenda are prepared in advance by these persons. Minutes are kept and taken by the lawyers. Members of the boards are permitted to see the minutes only at subsequent meetings with little opportunity to review them. [These] minutes have at times been rewritten and/or fabricated by [Davis associates] with the intent to maintain [their] control over the associations. [And] routinely, the board of directors is informed of action taken by the attorneys *after the fact*... no matters of any great importance are ever presented to the board for decision."[13]

Davis insisted upon complete control and refused to tolerate criticism. One of his opponents was Executive Director William Fitch. Their long-simmering feud boiled over when Ethel Andrus asked Fitch to fire an employee she suspected of stealing. The person in question was a Davis hire. Davis was furious. "Soon after that," Fitch recalled, "Dr. Andrus had all of us in Washington out to dinner one evening, along with Leonard. Leonard walked me off to the side as we were coming back from dinner, and he said, 'Bill, how could you let this happen?' My comment was 'Look, Leonard, how could you let it happen? He was your friend.' Leonard's comment at that time has stuck with me ever since. It was: 'I think you've outlived your usefulness as far as I'm concerned.'"[14] Not long after that, Andrus "decided" that the AARP should have five executive directors instead of one—an all too obvious infringement on Fitch's territory.

Davis had one of the sweetest sweetheart deals in American business history, and he knew it. For instance, AARP presidents, sometimes unwittingly, were used as pitchmen for Davis's increasing array of "services" by "signing" all AARP insurance come-ons. Alice VanLandingham was furious when she found out by chance that Davis, without her consent, had been putting her name on all kinds of solicitations.

Colonial Penn's cozy arrangement with AARP was bringing in mountains of money—80 percent of Colonial Penn's profits came from the AARP monopoly.

This horrified then-AARP public relations official Lloyd Wright. "Here were these people—wonderful people, I am sure," he recalled, "who had worked their way up through the rolls of volunteer leaders to become president. And they were being positioned to the membership as pitchmen for insurance. They had no idea."[15]

In promoting the group insurance health insurance plan as a "service" rather than a profit-making enterprise, Davis had another advantage: an unpaid volunteer sales force. In more than two thousand chapters across the nation, volunteers promoted Davis's insurance policies. Chapters were forbidden to mention the name of Colonial Penn's competitors. Chapter bylaws said that members could not be offered "any commodities or services already offered by the association."

Each chapter was required to form an insurance committee "to provide information about AARP Group Health Insurance Plans and the AARP-recommended insurance policies." In other words, their real job was to provide unpaid labor for Davis and Colonial Penn. "As Leonard Davis came to realize, the chapters had many useful purposes," said David Jeffreys, the AARP official who organized the early chapters.[16] "They were an avenue through which you could send a speaker to talk about insurance, to talk about travel service and various other services the association was developing in those days, all of which were operated by various entities of Mr. Davis. So they became very vital parts of the organization."

Whatever function the AARP had, Colonial Penn was there. This made people uncomfortable. "Colonial Penn was a major trauma," recalled staffer Mary Chenoweth, who oversaw the volunteers for a large area in the Northeast.[17] "Colonial Penn had staff that went to all of the area leadership meetings and practically all of the chapter workshops that we had. They were everywhere." And did they push their products? "Oh my yes!" replied Chenoweth. "They gave presentations—that's what they were there for."

Colonial Penn's cozy arrangement with AARP was bringing in mountains of money—80 percent of Colonial Penn's profits came from the AARP monopoly. And since members trusted "their" association, they didn't shop around or complain, thus allowing Colonial Penn to charge premiums and offer benefits out of sync with the market. In short, AARP customers got the short end of the stick. In 1974, for instance, while other commercial insurers paid out 90.6 cents in benefits for every dollar they took in premiums, Colonial Penn paid out only 61.9 cents in benefits for every dollar received.

As might be expected, Colonial Penn was growing rapidly. Author Charles Morris calculated that in the decade from 1967 to 1976, Colonial Penn's revenues "had grown a stunning tenfold, from $46 million to $445 million, for an annual growth rate of almost 30 percent. Almost all of its revenues—92 percent of its health insurance revenues—came from NRTA/AARP members."

LEONARD DAVIS COULDN'T CONTROL everything. In January 1976 two devastating reports on the AARP's business side brought down the wrath of AARP's suddenly enlightened seniors. The first bombshell appeared in *Forbes* magazine. Ironically, Colonial Penn wasn't the focus in this story, an exhaustive study of the 1970–75 earnings records of more than a thousand U.S. companies with revenues of more than $250 million each. However, many readers were stunned to see Colonial Penn at the head of a list that included such giants as General Electric, IBM, General Dynamics, and Mobil. In fact, *Forbes* reported, the Colonial Penn Group was the most profitable company in the United States.

Also that January, the highly respected *Consumer Reports*

dropped the second bombshell when it reported that AARP members were getting lousy service from Colonial Penn.[18] This blew the lid off the sweetheart deal. The article reported that the Consumers Union had found that, out of sixteen prominent health insurance policies for the elderly, Colonial Penn's AARP policy offered the "least protection." Moreover, the article implied, AARP members were being duped.

Colonial Penn and the AARP fought back. Acting AARP executive director Harriet Miller, not yet on the road to rebellion, wrote AARP's leadership a soothing memo. In it she stated that "both the association and Colonial Penn have always exercised autonomy in their own domains." Miller was rolled out by Davis to utter the same line to a skittish Baltimore firm that had just invested heavily in Colonial Penn.

At the same time, AARP–Davis lawyers were mobilizing a campaign to stop *Consumer Reports* from issuing reprints of the article. "Colonial Penn is attempting, through the implied threat of a lawsuit, to prevent us from distributing a reprint," editor Irwin Landau wrote in an internal memo.[19] Landau later elaborated: "Colonial Penn, through telephone calls from its president and letters from its legal counsel, alleged that we had deliberately failed to publish some shady stuff about its main competitor.... We finally found it necessary to publish a long—and tedious—follow-up responding to each of Colonial Penn's points."[20]

But despite all defensive efforts by Davis and company, a snowball effect had begun. *Forbes* followed up with an article headlined: "Colonial Penn Group and the AARP have an unusual relationship: You might call it incestuous." *Forbes* indicated that the lack of competitive bidding almost certainly assured a bad deal for AARP members. [21]

The media reports apparently burst the bubble: AARP members began to criticize their organization. A convention of retired teachers in Hawaii resolved that steps should be taken to guarantee that insurance contracts should be awarded on a competitive basis. And state insurance commissioners across the country began to notice an increase in complaints about Colonial Penn products, many of them from AARP members.

Newly awakened members weren't the AARP's only big problem. The U.S. Postal Service also woke from its long slumber. They began a full-scale investigation of the AARP, news of which broke in the nationally syndicated column of Jack Anderson. Anderson reported: "They suspect the nonprofit group may be a front for improperly peddling insurance to the elderly by using mail subsidies that cost the taxpayers an estimated $10 million a year."[22] According to an internal Postal Service memo in the fall of 1977, officials believed that AARP and Colonial Penn had "less than an arm's length" relationship that did not "comport with accepted standards of business practice." The postal memo stated that "the primary purpose of the organizations could very well be to serve as the marketing agents of Colonial Penn Group." Anderson surmised that much of Colonial Penn's profits depended on the special nonprofit mailing rates. It saved AARP and Colonial Penn at least five cents per solicitation. Multiply that by the 192 million solicitations they sent out in 1977, and you get a staggering total: more than $9 million in savings.

AARP tried to shrug off the Postal Service investigation. The association insisted to members and journalists that it was a routine matter, something that was done all the time. But Arthur Cahn, the Postal Services assistant general counsel who initiated the probe, said otherwise. The investigation continued for four years and included 5,600 complaints, testimonies from senior citizens, and other documents that filled more than eighteen cabinet drawers. Cahn, who was transferred mid-investigation, told a *Washington Post* reporter that the Postal Service had "more than enough" to show that AARP was a marketing agent for Colonial Penn.[23]

American taxpayers and regular businesses were, in effect, subsidizing Colonial Penn. In 1981 the Postal Service recommended that the U.S. district attorney pursue a criminal fraud action against Colonial Penn and the AARP, but no action was taken on the grounds that it would be almost impossible to prove criminal intent.

Davis might have held on to the AARP if not for Executive Director Harriet Miller. Miller began to resent Colonial Penn's "advisors."

Sensing trouble, Davis moved quickly. On Sunday, October 2, 1977, he personally fired Miller. AARP President Alice VanLandingham remembered the firing this way: "On Saturday and Sunday before the fall board meeting, the honorary presidents (Davis and Lana) interviewed each member of the executive committee individually and convinced them that Harriet was unfit and they had letters to prove same—which were ridiculous and shameful. They grilled me for hours and I never agreed with them. I told them that Harriet had been hassled into frustration and that no administrator could ever succeed under that kind of stress."

> "They suspect the nonprofit group may be a front for improperly peddling insurance to the elderly by using mail subsidies that cost the taxpayers an estimated $10 million a year."

Miller was replaced by Cy Brickfield, a hand-picked member of Davis's inner circle. Interestingly, Brickfield stepped into the job at a salary of $80,000—up $20,000 from Miller's $60,000 salary. He immediately began negotiating with Miller about her severance. At first, she almost settled for one year's salary, spread over a two-year period, but then backed out. When she threatened a lawsuit, Brickfield thought she was bluffing.

He was wrong. On May 2, 1978, Miller filed a $4 million suit against the AARP. Her twenty-seven–page complaint was devastating. A sample:

> AARP, which presents the illusion of a voluntary, nonprofit membership organization unselfishly representing the interests of older people, actually constitutes an integral element in the vast profit-making empire of Leonard Davis....
>
> The fact is that AARP was designed and created to be a group for insurance purposes. The thorough and extensive trappings of a membership organization actually constitute a convenient and effective cover for the profit-making purposes for which the Associations' trusting members are used....
>
> Through a series of brilliantly designed and skillfully executed strategies, the Association has been systematically deprived of the

governance of its own affairs.... By controlling information, communications, finances, sources of legal counsel, and the actions of a
large number of people through intimidation, economic pressure,
and guile, Leonard Davis and his associates have been able to create
and maintain a gigantic show-window which to the public, including many Association members and employees, displays many
programs and services which appear to serve the interests of older
people. Behind the facade, however, is the hidden reality of the
personal profit and the power which Leonard Davis unconscionably
wields in totalitarian fashion to maintain his control and enlarge his
fortune while bending the Association to his purposes....

NOT SURPRISINGLY, THE PRESS PICKED UP the controversy. Andy
Rooney, then an investigative reporter for *60 Minutes*, did the piece
that signaled the end of the Davis regime. Titled "Super-Salesman,"
Rooney's segment hit all the crucial points in the AARP–Colonial
Penn arrangement. In introducing the piece, Morley Safer noted
that, while many businesses were discovering that older Americans
were a lucrative market for all kinds of goods, "no businessman has
taken better advantage of it than a super-salesman named Leonard
Davis." The report was a direct hit. An "insurance counselor" (a volunteer) for an AARP chapter was shown as hawking Colonial Penn
insurance; for her efforts, she got a box of candy once a year. It was
clear that most AARP members were totally in the dark about the
relationship between Colonial Penn and "their" association.

AARP staffers and volunteers were caught off guard. Most had
not realized the extent of Davis's involvement. Myra Herrick, a staff
director of volunteers in the Northeast, recalled that "things were
really going downhill and [the Washington office] was spending
more time defending than getting anything done."

Finally even Davis knew he had to go. But he didn't walk, he was
shoved—and by his very own lawyers, acting with Cy Brickfield. In
February 1979 the lawyers, by way of signaling Davis's end, cannily
noted that the Colonial Penn contract would expire in mid-1981.
They put a resolution before the board to open up the insurance

business to competitive bidding. Not only did the resolution pass, the board rescinded the right of the two honorary presidents, Leonard Davis and Ruth Lana, to attend board meetings "other than by invitation."[24]

MANY LEFTOVER PROBLEMS still had to be resolved. Among them were a half-dozen lawsuits against the AARP and Colonial Penn. "Everybody was suing us for something," said AARP President Olaf Kaasa.[25] The AARP realized it was time to end all the suits, among them Harriet Miller's. So in November 1980, just before the trial was to begin, AARP agreed to pay Miller $480,000. One of the things AARP bought was Miller's silence. The case record was sealed.

Today, AARP tries to forget Leonard Davis, who lives, a multi-millionaire, in Palm Springs. His name is never uttered, and his portrait, which once hung at headquarters, has been banished to oblivion. He is the AARP's invisible man. Except for one thing: AARP is still dependent on product sales for its survival. The Faustian bargain lives on.

CHAPTER 7

The Big Sell

I sincerely believe that AARP should receive a Nobel Prize—for hucksterism. They are a sorry self-serving outfit, and practically useless as a spokesman for seniors.

—Timothy Pearson, former AARP member,
Santa Rosa, California[1]

I was invited to join the AARP. In all honesty, I'm a bit disappointed with AARP since joining. They seem more like a sales organization than anything else.

—John J. Gralenski, AARP member,
Gorham, New Hampshire[2]

The secret of AARP's riches is in more than two dozen "member service" products it promotes to its members every year. The "member services" revenue equals about $5.3 billion of the total revenue—with a couple hundred million dollars in loose change additionally coming from membership dues, federal grants, and advertising revenue, in that order. AARP members may pay just $8 in membership fees each year, but the real annual figure over which the AARP accountants salivate is the $150 that the average member spends each year on AARP products. The revenue the AARP generates from selling to members is so sizeable that some might well argue there shouldn't be any membership dues at all, that AARP should give away memberships just to build up the list of potential customers.

AARP is required by the Internal Revenue Service to report income it receives from membership dues, federal grants, and other sources. But the AARP need only report the "administrative allowance" and "royalties" it collects from insurance and other products it sells—not the amount that members pay for these items. This is a useful loophole for the AARP, because it allows them to keep confidential the staggering amount of money they and corporate business partners receive from the members. Still, I have estimated that the total revenue for the AARP and its partners in 1994 was $5.6 billion. However, it should be noted that the AARP's for-profit business partners pay tax on their profits. If the AARP were a for-profit corporation, it would have been in the top half of the Fortune 500 that year. Indeed, it would have been larger than General Dynamics, Bethlehem Steel, Corning, Black & Decker, Wells Fargo, Boise Cascade, Maytag, Upjohn, Hershey Foods, and Union Carbide. AARP pulls in more revenue every year than Avon. It is bigger than TWA, railroads like Norfolk Southern and Southern Pacific, and the huge Chiquita Brands food conglomerate. Media empires like Gannett, Turner Broadcasting, Los Angeles–based Times-Mirror, and the CBS network don't come close to AARP's income.

AARP OFFICIALS EXPLAIN they are just trying to help the members out—and the enormous revenue they derive is only incidental. The publicly-released "Where We Stand" position paper asks "Why is AARP involved in selling products and services to members?" There is a high-sounding explanation: "We recognize the need for products designed to meet the specific needs of the older population. These products/services include emergency road service, group travel services, specially designed automobile and home insurance, group health insurance, an investment program, and a nonprofit mail service pharmacy."[3] But "AARP does not sell any service or product." If the AARP doesn't "sell" any service or product, what exactly does it do? "We do endorse certain services which the association seeks to have developed for AARP members," the position paper explains.

It is often the case with the AARP that it bends the truth to make itself appear benevolent. Technically, it is true that the AARP has hired an array of generally blue-chip companies to manufacture, sell, and service the products. For example, Prudential Insurance Company of America underwrites and does the heavy-duty work on the group health insurance plan, while ITT Hartford does the same for auto and home insurance products. But AARP officials are so intimately involved with these "service providers" that the claim they don't "sell" but only "endorse" is an understatement. AARP uses computer-generated programs that identify which members are most likely to buy the products, and gives that to their business partners. AARP staffers train the "service providers" on how best to approach their members. AARP spends a mini-fortune on annual surveys to find out if members are satisfied with the products, and what would persuade them to buy more. (In fact, AARP solicits members at least twenty times more for product sales than for their opinions on proposed legislation.) AARP hawks the products at all its conventions. And the most prominent and pervasive advertisements in its two all-membership publications are for AARP products, and no competitor is allowed to advertise or is likely to be mentioned in the editorial copy of those publications. But AARP does far more than just lend its name to the products of business partners.

Without these products, and the revenue kicked back from their sales to the AARP in the form of an "administrative allowance" and "royalties," the AARP might cease to exist in less than five years. Knowing this, the AARP can be credited by other businessmen for making two historically successful mass-marketing decisions. The first came in the early 1980s, when AARP dropped the membership age from fifty-five to fifty. This pulled millions more "prospects" into AARP's dues and product-solicitation universe. The second slick marketing move has been to keep the dues low, thus enticing more people to walk into the AARP store. "Since AARP's very low annual dues are basically promotional, the override on services bought by members has become an increasingly important chunk of revenues," *Forbes* observed.[4] The *Los Angeles Times* came to the same conclusion: "Keeping the dues low is an excellent tactic. Once members are enrolled, the AARP can sell them mutual funds, health insurance, life insurance and prescription drugs. In fact, the organization makes more money from its products and services than the cash it collects from membership dues."[5]

The AARP's top staff officials claim that membership dues are still the largest source of the AARP's income. If they admit otherwise, the AARP would be in violation of its own board of directors dictum that mandates member dues remain the dominant revenue source. So how does AARP justify this pretense when, for example in 1994, the products and services unquestionably earned them a net income of $173.3 million—or half their nongrant revenue—while member dues were less, $145.7 million? They simply say that the group health insurance program "administrative allowance" and related interest earnings, which accounted for $119.4 million of the sales net, is a different kind of money than all the other products they sell. By distinguishing between the different kinds of insurance monies, they can say membership dues is the biggest source of revenue, group health insurance comes second, and all the other products together come third.

Members who discover the AARP is making a King Midas fortune often experience a feeling of shock, followed quickly by a sense of betrayal. Virginia Fine, once a California AARP chapter officer who dared to look into AARP's coffers, resigned after concluding "it's no more than a big business. The whole Washington operation is simply geared toward making money."[6]

AARP staff know the organization has a pristine nonprofit image with its members. The natural presumption of such trusting souls is that the AARP would endorse and promote the best products on the market, because its motto is to serve, not to be served. Most don't know that the AARP will seldom inform them about the better deals that are out there, because that does not serve the AARP's revenue interest.

"Members doubtless assume that [AARP] acts as a disinterested arranger of the services they endorse," Consumer Reports once pointedly observed.[7] But members "should be aware that the endorsement... reflects a cozy commercial relationship, not a disinterested selection among similar services that may be available." When it was explained to her by a reporter, seventy-three-year-old Arie Cary of Miami said she had "some misgivings about that. After all, they palm themselves off as a nonprofit group dedicated to helping seniors. Yet they're making money when they could be dropping prices for services instead."[8]

> **The AARP is big business, taking advantage of a huge tax loophole by officially being recognized as a non-profit organization.**

One member filed a class action suit against AARP in 1995. Joseph Schiff, a retired doctor living in the Chicago suburbs, filed the civil suit in the Superior Court of the District of Columbia. He charged that AARP had violated the D.C. Consumer Protection Procedures Act (CPPA) by "misrepresenting the reasons for offering, and the prices charged on, the goods and services it provides."[9] His official complaint further read: "This is a class action brought by plaintiff on his own behalf and on behalf of all AARP members... for violations of CPPA, common law fraud and unjust enrichment. In particular, AARP misrepresented to and misled plaintiff and the class into believing that AARP is a nonprofit membership organization whose purpose is to serve the interests of persons 50 years or older when, in reality, it is designed to and has earned enormous profits of unrelated business income, has paid extraordinary salaries to and otherwise benefitted its officers and directors."

Schiff's lawyer, Roy Goldberg, testified in a Congressional hearing that "the crux of the complaint is that, while the AARP has pretended to be a nonprofit organization with the purported objective of helping its elderly membership, the reality is that the AARP is using its members to generate millions of dollars in profits. Dr. Schiff contends that the AARP engaged in a massive deception about what it really is and what it does with the money it gets from members."[10]

AARP headquarters should have been at least a bit chagrined, instead of feeling victorious, when Associate Judge Geoffrey M. Alprin granted AARP's motion to dismiss on a technicality in May 1995. Judge Alprin cited legal precedent for determining that the consumer protection act could not be applied "to corporate 'merchants' whose status is nonprofit."[11] Which means, of course, that the AARP was free, in Dr. Schiff's view, to misrepresent itself to its members, while at the same time hiding under the nonprofit cloak. In a second reason for dismissal, Judge Alprin ruled that AARP didn't have to tell the members anything about their business revenue: "Plaintiff (Dr. Schiff) has not called this court's attention to any requirement that AARP has a duty to disclose the fact that some of its activities generate a significant amount of business income... without such a duty the failure to disclose as alleged by plaintiff is simply not a basis for a fraud action." Dr. Joseph Schiff and other members who have complained about AARP's big sell have raised a legitimate question: Does AARP have more concern for the bottom line than for its members?

THE ENORMOUS BUSINESS AARP conducts in conjunction with corporate partners creates a significant conflict of interest—one that inevitably taints its lobbying operation. Nowhere is that conflict more pronounced than with AARP's $120-million-a-year health insurance partnership with Prudential, America's largest insurance company. AARP's piece of the rock is a big one, and this has not escaped the attention of more alert members. "It appears to me that AARP is a Trojan horse for the insurance industry—since Prudential is one of the major health care players—and it is short-changing the senior citizens it's supposed to represent," said member Charles A. Casey of Norwalk, Connecticut.[12] In Belmont, California, John Stoddard, an AARP member for twenty years and a past chapter president and legislative chairman, concluded: "I believe AARP national [staff] is overly influenced by the large amount of money that insurance premiums bring in. So they are not looking out for the best interests of seniors on health care reform."[13]

The members have not been the only ones to take notice of this. The respected *National Journal* observed that "mixing business and advocacy has potential pitfalls. The AARP opens itself to questions of whether its public policy positions may be guided by business considerations rather than seniors' interests."[14] House Chief *Deputy* Majority Whip J. Dennis Hastert was quoted by the *Journal* in 1995 as saying those who dealt with the AARP on Capitol Hill were cognizant that their lobbyists "have a vested interest—they have some big businesses that they're tied up in."[15] Even natural allies of the liberally-oriented AARP are wary about the overshadowing private health insurance conflict. The labor union–based National Council of Senior Citizens (NCSC) has not forgotten they had to fight the Colonial Penn–run AARP three decades ago to get Medicare enacted in the first place. "We still view them primarily as a marketing organization," explained one NCSC official.

One of AARP's big businesses is "Medigap" policies that cover costs not covered by Medicare. In 1989–90 there were congressional efforts to reform Medigap policies. AARP saw "reform" as an opportunity to eliminate competition. As journalist Ron Suskind recalls, "There were companies that were eating into their Medigap business just because they were providing better policies, cheaper. AARP was incensed about this because, my God, there's rent to pay on that headquarters. So they initiated strong consumer-based pressure for action on Capitol Hill."[16] What happened next is spelled out in Suskind's 1993 article in *Smart Money:*

> AARP turned its powerful lobbying machine on an issue very close to home: reforming all Medigap policies. There was well-documented fraud in the Medigap system, with unscrupulous agents selling duplicative policies to unwitting seniors. AARP, using its rapid-deployment research operation, offered a study showing that 24 percent of seniors had more than one Medigap policy. In November 1990, Congress passed a bill to reform and standardize Medigap.
>
> The law said companies could offer only 10 standardized types of Medigap policies. Over the next nine months, a core advisory

committee made up of representatives from six consumer groups and six insurance companies met to help craft those 10 plans. On the consumer group side was AARP. On the company side was Prudential. "Considering the conflicts, let's just say it was all a little sticky," says Gail Shearer, manager of policy analysis for Consumers Union and co-chair of the advisory committee.

The result was a little sticky as well. "Instead of eliminating fraud through better regulation, the reforms eliminated free choice, giving everyone the same plain-vanilla offerings," says Martin Weiss, president of Weiss Research Inc., a firm that rates the financial health of insurance companies. Since then, a number of AARP's rivals have dropped out of business, and others are struggling. While AARP concedes it has benefitted from reform, it insists driving out the competition was not its aim.[17]

AARP OFFICIALS POINT to their efforts on health care reform as proof that they serve seniors rather than the insurance industry. But none of AARP's lobbying endangered any income from the Prudential–AARP partnership. Here's the sequence:

Throughout the early 1990s, AARP spent millions of dollars holding forums and conducting polls to construct a health care reform plan AARP members would support. The result was an AARP plan unveiled in 1993 that inevitably represented only a minority of AARP members. Called "Health Care America," it essentially proposed raising taxes to give Medicare to every American. That, of course, would create a universal, instead of seniors-only, need for Medigap insurance. While John Rother said the "insurance companies are dead set against us [AARP] on this one," a spokesman for Prudential said AARP's plan didn't "upset" them because "there would be a need, a great need, I think, for supplemental coverage of the type we're now providing."[18]

A top official with the nonprofit consumer organization United Seniors Health Cooperative confirms the point emphatically: "AARP came out with a plan for health reform which has Medicare for everybody. Now what does that mean? It means Medigap for everybody. It's a huge business interest. Prudential could not have advised a more favorable business than Medicare for everybody. You think it's just a coincidence that AARP supported a plan that would double their business? In what way was AARP's public policy any different than Prudential's public policy? That's the story. AARP has not supported alliances or anything that would hurt Prudential. Now, if I were getting more than $100 million a year, I wouldn't rock the boat either."

Members who discover the AARP is making a King Midas fortune often experience a feeling of shock, followed quickly by a sense of betrayal.

Bruce Vladeck, the Clinton-appointed administrator of the Health Care Financing Administration (which administers Medicare), reassured AARP at its biannual 1994 convention that if Clinton-style health care reform passed, it wouldn't damage the AARP–Prudential relationship. A New Jersey member asked during the Q&A period if he would still be paying for a Medigap Prudential/AARP policy under Clinton care. "I can tell you that we expect your relationship will remain essentially the same," Vladeck said soothingly. "The co-insurance and deductibles and other things for which your supplemental policy pays will still be in the Medicare program, and you'll still probably want that supplemental policy."[19]

Of all the health care reform plans, only the so-called "single payer" plan—where the government pays most of the bills—would have seriously damaged the private health insurance industry. Sidney Wolfe, who founded the Public Citizen Health Research Group with Ralph Nader, strongly felt the single-payer plan would have provided the best security for AARP's elderly members, and accused AARP of selling out to Prudential.[20]

Many AARP members felt similarly. The California wing of AARP actually fought for a single-payer ballot initiative.

A staff attorney from Wolfe's consumer group, Sara Nichols, taking private notes in a White House meeting on health care reform, caught AARP's top lobbyist, John Rother, making an embarrassing confession. "During this meeting with Ira Magaziner, John Rother said, 'Well, there's good news and bad news. The bad news is a majority of our AARP members support single payer. The good news is we think we can get them to swallow managed competition.' I thought it was a fairly cynical way to deal with their membership."[21] Especially since, publicly, AARP claimed that only a small minority of its members supported the single-payer proposal.

Health insurance isn't AARP's only business. AARP is a corporate fat cat but it has been sometimes more successful at hyping itself than selling products. It has had some serious commercial failures:

THE ROADPHONE: In March 1994 a senior staffer briefed a special Board committee on the exciting prospects of Roadphone, a product offered by a San Jose, California–based company, ASCNet.[22] For AARP's elderly members, it was a simple device with only three buttons. One would dial the nearest 911; a second, the nearest road service for breakdown assistance; and the third, a Roadphone operator to place outgoing personal calls. The special phone would cost members $129.95, and an additional $55 payable in advance for the first year's service.

The AARP would receive $5 for each phone sold, which amounted to a cheap sale of their membership list. The first test was in Billings, Montana. ASCNet was given the list of 9,878 active AARP households. They were thrilled to sell 59 phones in the first month—what they called "0.6% market penetration."[23] The next test was in San Diego, where Roadphone got to give a sales pitch to 29,171 AARP members.[24] More tests were planned for Providence, Rhode Island, and upper New York State. But before that happened, Roadphone went dead.

By September, ASCNet was bankrupt. At least four hundred San Diego AARP members and one hundred Billings members lost about $200 apiece. They had their Roadphones, but they couldn't work off a defunct network. They had been personally solicited, they felt, by Executive Director Horace Deets who had written them the previous July urging: "I think you'll find this new service to be of great value." Eighty-one-year-old member Miriam McIver couldn't believe that AARP refused to reimburse her. She wrote Deets: "I'm sure I don't need to remind you that the majority of AARP's members are elderly and are on a very limited budget. A $200 loss represents a very real hardship."

AARP responded that it couldn't afford to pay back the five hundred AARP members who were left holding a useless Roadphone. Instead, AARP suggested its members contact their credit card company to withhold payment or get a reimbursement.[25] "It was important not to take the responsibility for their [ASCNet] going bankrupt [because] there is always the potential for litigation in this," Deets offered in one explanation.[26] "This is a very litigious society, as we know. And the primary obligation was on the company that provided the phone." He did add months later, belatedly, that they "stood ready to reimburse those who were not reimbursed" through the credit card companies—but this was stated only after damaging publicity made their nonreimbursement policy a disaster.

AARP Federal Credit Union: AARP's announcement in early 1988 that it was going to form a federal credit union caused quite a stir. "Much of what the Association touches turns to gold," proclaimed a *Washington Post* article, predicting great financial rewards for "AARP Federal."[27] Journalists, bankers, industry insiders, and AARP officials thought that this time the organization with more than twenty-five million members had truly found the ultimate pot of gold.

Recently-retired Executive Director Cyril Brickfield became chairman of the board. A former staffer for Indiana Senator Birch Bayh, P.A. Mack, headed up the operation, and a financial journalist, Laura Rossman, was hired as vice president. The "service provider" was a Fortune 500 company, Bank One of Columbus, Ohio. They did the back-office work for the three basic services AARP Federal provided: a savings account, a Visa credit card, and a cash access card.

Fearing they would lose considerable business to AARP Federal, bankers launched an all-out war on Capitol Hill. Banking lobbyists urged lawmakers to take away AARP's nonprofit, tax-exempt status.

Bankers wanted AARP Federal to pay taxes and operate under the same rules they did. AARP held firm, maintaining that their credit union was a "member-owned" financial institution that just happened to have a much larger group of people from which to draw than other credit unions. Indeed, the scope and potential size of AARP Federal was larger than anything of its kind that had ever been tried.

Like the banks, other credit unions feared losing business to AARP Federal. Worse, if lawmakers decided to take away AARP's tax-exempt status, all credit unions would likely be forced to operate under new rules.

These objections notwithstanding, the potential windfall for AARP seemed to be boundless. "In terms of brand power," wrote bank marketing consultant Michael P. Sullivan in an American Banker editorial, "I predict the AARP Federal Credit Union will become one of the best-known nationwide names in the financial services industry within the next five years."[28]

How could AARP Federal not succeed? If just 3 percent of the association's members signed on, the credit union would become the nation's largest within five years. By the end of 1989, AARP officials predicted, the credit union would have a staggering $4.2 billion in assets, including some $1.7 billion in savings accounts.[29] Yet, two short years later, AARP Federal folded. By the end of 1989 the credit union's assets were a mere $150 million—a far cry from the $4.2 billion that had been predicted.

What happened?

In order to keep operational costs down, AARP decided not to open any regional branches—all transactions would take place through the mail, over the phone, or at automated teller machines. This proved to be a fatal mistake. "Generally, elderly people are particularly resistant to that kind of a relationship with a financial institution," says Bob Loftus, director of the National Credit Union Administration's public affairs office.[30] Seniors were used to dealing with tellers at local banks and were reluctant to give up the personal service.

AARP also offered fewer services than most banks. Only several thousand AARP members ever signed up for AARP Federal.

As the failed credit union venture demonstrates, AARP's millions of members won't buy just anything that's peddled to them. Its members, perhaps much to AARP's chagrin, can—and often do—think for themselves.

AARP Travel Service: The saddest of AARP's failed business ventures has been their once-pioneering travel service. As old as AARP itself, tours for the elderly were a long-cherished dream of founder Ethel Andrus. "We decided we should give the (AARP) members something to think about besides just their health," remembered Ruth Lana.[31] She was appointed to head up the nascent travel service which was designed, according to an Andrus write-up in 1958, to be the "modern, smart way to see the world, with all the problems of scheduling, reservations, routing, baggage, etc., miraculously lifted from your shoulders. Budget-priced in addition, courier-escorted from morn till night, we offer it to you with the proud assurance of responsibility."[32]

> **The enormous business AARP conducts in conjuction with corporate partners creates a significant conflict of interest—one that inevitably taints its lobbying operation.**

Lana laughed years afterward at how little she knew about the travel business at the time. "Why did I inherit it? I didn't even know where South America was, really, you know." She advertised in the first issue of *Modern Maturity* that AARP would host between 250 and 300 people in groups of 25 on tours of Europe.

Eventually, after a false start, a new subsidiary corporation was formed under the auspices of Colonial Penn, named Grand Circle Travel. Colonial Penn paid AARP up to $25 for every member who joined a trip. In return, AARP agreed to devote at least two pages of every issue of *Modern Maturity* to "news" about Grand Circle travel tours.[33] Lana went on the Colonial Penn/Grand Circle payroll.

Today, when retirees dominate the travel market, it is hard to imagine that Ruth Lana was breaking new ground. Travel agents back then stayed away from the senior business, thinking the elderly were too picky, too frail, and too timid for world travel. Lana thought that was nonsense. While she had no training in the travel business, she knew the senior business. Retirees would travel as long as the tour provider ensured that hotels had elevators, and arranged easier schedules with long stays, short bus rides, frequent stops, and additional porters.

Lana's personal touch permeated the AARP travel business. She even produced a "Happy Travelers" songbook replete with much-requested favorites like "After the Ball," "Aunt Dinah's Quilting Party," "Hail! Hail! The Gang's All Here," "Over There," and "Let Me Call You Sweetheart."[34] It fit in one's pocket, and it made it seem like "we were just one big happy family," remembered AARP volunteer leader Robert Utzinger.[35] "And there was Ruth up there leading the singing and I thought, 'Boy, what a great organization this is.' They had a lot of feeling, a lot of spirit."

But when AARP finally broke with Colonial Penn as an insurance provider, Grand Circle Travel was one of the casualties. AARP canceled its travel arrangement with Grand Circle. Lana made a heartbreaking decision—to stay with Colonial Penn and its travel subsidiary instead of going back to the AARP staff.

In 1982 AARP signed its travel business over to Olson Travelworld and told Grand Circle it could no longer advertise in AARP publications. Olson had a lock on that. With substantial resources already sunk in the senior travel market, Grand Circle couldn't afford to lose *Modern Maturity* as an advertising outlet, so Colonial Penn sued AARP for "unlawful competition." The suit was settled out of court, but Grand Circle was never allowed to advertise in AARP publications again.

Ultimately, the AARP–Olson partnership was a costly failure. Olson was owned by quixotic Illinois multimillionaire David Elmore, who had quietly built up a travel business empire by buying respected firms. For AARP, he created a separate corporate entity, the AARP Travel Service, which went bankrupt by 1990.

The AARP's much-vaunted travel business never recovered from the embarrassment of the Olson fiasco. A knowledgeable senior official said AARP lost about $17 million—at least $10 million of which went to members for canceled tours and lost money.

AARP sued Elmore and received condominiums in Vail, Colorado, as compensation.

Desperate to recover the lost ground, AARP signed a new contract with American Express in late 1990 to run a new service, AARP Travel Experience. But American Express lost hundreds of thousands of dollars on the joint venture every year; and after four years of failure, American Express told AARP it was bailing out. AARP charged them $500,000 for the privilege of breaking the losing contract, and assigned the Travel Program staff to other positions.

CHAPTER 8

Drugs and the AARP

I wrote [the AARP] and asked them why their prices were higher than the drug store when they are supposed to be an organization that saves money for elderly people. I wrote two letters and they would never answer either one of the letters.

—Jerry M. Cooke, Radcliff, Kentucky[1]

I joined AARP in 1981. I tried their so-called money-saving programs and quit them all. For instance, I ran a check on their prescription drug prices and it was another big lie. I get a better deal with my hometown drug store.

—John Rozsa, Rockville, Indiana[2]

The AARP Pharmacy Service is the second-oldest in AARP's constellation of money-making businesses, and it has ballooned to such proportions as to control 10 percent of the entire mail-ordering market.

Started in 1959, the pharmacy service was the brainchild of Ethel Percy Andrus, the altruist, and Leonard Davis, the capitalist. Ruth Lana recalled "seeing these letters, pitiful letters, that came across her [Andrus's] desk where they'd say, 'I can only buy half of the prescription. I can't afford to buy all the prescription.' Every time Dr. Andrus heard something like that she tried to solve it."

Andrus approached Davis for ideas. Davis remembered talking with her about "the problems of the costs of medications. I said that I thought it might be conceivable that we could create a mail order pharmacy operation, and that by doing that, we could save people considerable amounts of money."[3]

The "AARP Drug Buying Service" was initially a one-man one-room operation in Washington, D.C. Its one registered pharmacist not only filled the prescriptions, but also personally dropped them off at the post office on his way home.

The service might have died if not for the arrival of Herbert Haft, a pharmacist who in World War II was an army supply officer, handling huge shipments. After the war, he started what would become the Dart Drug chain. "I was the first discounter in the United States, before Wal-Mart and K-Mart came along," he says.[4]

Haft was such a pioneer that he was offering discounts when it was illegal to do so. "Fair trade" laws made it illegal to sell prescription drugs well below the manufacturer's suggested retail price. As Haft expanded Dart Drug to sell other items at cut-rate prices, he became the defendant in more than one hundred antidiscount lawsuits filed against him by most of the major pharmaceutical companies and other companies like General Electric. Haft generally lost the cases, but he appealed them. Finally, in 1960, the Supreme Court ruled in his favor in a case filed by Parke-Davis, the huge pharmaceutical concern. "One of the things the Supreme Court ruling says is that an overwhelming majority of people, if asked, would rather pay $6 than $10 for Parke-Davis vitamins," said Haft. The landmark decision struck down "fair trade" laws as nothing more than price-fixing.

The young crusading businessman came to Andrus's attention, and she invited him to lunch. She also invited Senator Estes Kefauver of Tennessee, the powerful chairman of the Senate Subcommittee on Antitrust and Monopoly who was about to hold hearings on high pharmaceutical prices. Kefauver and Andrus wanted Haft to help them battle the pharmaceutical companies. After some hesitation, Haft agreed.

Andrus and Haft became star witnesses for the Kefauver hearings which, in turn, became free advertisements for the AARP Pharmacy Service and Dart Drug. Andrus was featured prominently on the "Today" show, and in the *New York Times*, *Newsweek*, and *Life* magazine. The pharmacy service grew rapidly. When its first manager—a nonpharmicist recommended by Davis—was fired because Andrus suspected he was stealing from the company, Andrus leaned on her friend, Haft, to step in and save it. Haft steered the early pharmacy service through some rough patches. Parke-Davis refused to supply AARP with their brand-name drugs when they found Andrus was discounting them. Two dozen state pharmacy boards filed suit and used other methods to stop the mail-order pharmacy service cold. In one case, pharmacists in St. Petersburg, Florida, tried to close down an AARP drug store. The pharmacists told their distributors they wouldn't buy their products if they sold them to the AARP store. So AARP's St. Petersburg store had to import drugs from Georgia. When the Florida pharmacists leaned on the Georgia distributors, the AARP flew drugs in from Washington, D.C. The D.C. airlift finally defeated the pharmacists, and their ban was lifted—the first of many AARP successes.

When Haft resigned because building his own Dart Drug chain didn't leave him enough time for the AARP Pharmacy Service, he was replaced by John McHugh, the man who put the biggest personal stamp on the AARP Pharmacy Service.

McHugh began his career with the Peoples Drug Store chain in 1950 while still a student at George Washington University. He worked his way up from clerk to pharmacist, to store manager, to pharmaceutical buyer, and finally to professional service director of the ten-state chain. Along the way he was nominated president of the Maryland Pharmaceutical Association. When AARP approached him in 1962, McHugh had no intention of risking everything by going over to the fledgling mail-order pharmacy industry. But AARP courted him assiduously, and finally convinced him by saying that he would be president of his own company—a company serving all fifty states, not just ten. And the job represented a substantial increase in income.

The AARP Pharmacy Service grew prodigiously under John McHugh. In 1962 the pharmacy occupied a lone three-story building in Washington, D.C., employing 14 pharmacists who filled 250,000 prescriptions annually.[5] Thirty years later, when McHugh retired, the AARP pharmacy had thirteen facilities, 250 pharmacists, and was filling 8 million prescriptions a year.

McHugh capitalized on the already existing strengths of the service, including privacy, price, and home delivery. One AARP official explained it this way: "Say you're in South Dakota. The pharmacist is your brother-in-law, and you don't want to let him know you have crabs or that you're taking some other major medicine. You don't want it known because it's private. Your pharmacist charges you more anyway because in South Dakota there's no competition, and he can't buy in bulk for cheaper prices because he doesn't have enough customers. And also, in South Dakota, when you're snowed in, who wants to go out every month to refill your prescription for heart medicine when it can arrive at your door through the mail?"

Another big feature was that, from the beginning, the AARP Pharmacy Service required no prepayment. They trusted their members to pay the bill. Leonard Davis claimed credit for this. "The question was, do you mail the pharmaceutical products out first and have the people pay you later, or do you require payment in advance. It was my feeling that we were dealing with a remarkable public of people who I felt had great integrity. And it was extremely well-proven by the low—very, very, low—amount of nonpayments." McHugh also had faith in the elderly and reported that, right to the current day, "our bad debt ratio would be the envy of anybody that knew it, that was in the business." A knowledgeable source confirmed that the bad debt the pharmacy writes off annually has averaged a mere one-tenth of 1 percent.

McHugh also expanded the AARP Pharmacy Service's nonprescription lines. Only six pages of a typical eighty-page catalogue were devoted to prescription drugs. The rest hawked hosiery, wheelchairs, laxatives, toiletries, nail clippers, and other sundries—all of which account for 40 percent of the pharmacy's sales today. "About the only things we don't sell like other pharmacies are Pampers and birth control pills," one pharmacy official joked. The customers would like to see them sell even more items, according to the pharmacy's confidential tracking surveys. One asked "which products they would order from the pharmacy catalog if the product were available," and found that the respondents wanted gift items (29 percent), craft/hobby kits (19 percent), books (16 percent), and dietetic candy (12 percent).[6]

The pharmacy also has its own line of AARP-brand generic products, of which vitamins are the biggest sellers. They've been in this business since Ethel Percy Andrus visited a Philadelphia factory where a pill-maker observed, "This assembly line is for Vitamin C. The first 20 million that come off the line we will package and put the Squibb Vitamin C label on. The next 15 million will get the Eli Lilly. There's no reason why the next million to come off the line can't have the AARP label." Pharmacy ads in AARP publications regularly feature AARP generics with the tagline, "the only difference is price." AARP makes a "stress-fighting" vitamin formula; "vegetarian vitamins... using no animal derivatives"; AARP Formula 235 natural bulk laxative, "good tasting but completely starch free"; AARP Formula 239 Analgesic Ointment, whose "only significant difference" from Ben Gay is its "low, low price"; AARP Formula 287 Light Coated Aspirin, which compares to Bayer Aspirin except for "our low price," and so on.

The AARP estimates that about 10 percent of the elderly have to cut back on necessary items, such as food and heating fuel, to afford their medications.

One drawback of the pharmacy service, McHugh discovered when he arrived, was that it took too long for the customers to get their prescriptions. He instituted time-saving measures with a six-day turnaround as the goal—two days for the prescription to come by mail, two days to fill it, and two days to send it in the mail. When the U.S. Postal Service proved too sluggish, he switched delivery systems to the United Parcel Service (UPS). (In the past few years, the pharmacy sevice dropped UPS because their prices rose too steeply, and the Postal Service had become more reliable and swifter, in McHugh's opinion.)

Telemarketing is also important. Until 1993 the majority of pharmacy service orders came by mail. Now the majority of orders come through a toll-free number, linked to AARP's massive telemarketing machine. "Their pharmacy does give an excellent price," says Henry F. Sharp, a certified financial planner and AARP member living in Rehrersburg, Pennsylvania.[7] "However, even then, the operator will give other 'specials,' and as a result some senior citizens will purchase items really not needed!" A former AARP Pharmacy Service employee said that this was why he left the job. "I didn't like doing the telemarketing. The poor elderly were trying to pay for prescriptions, and we're trying to sell them shampoo or something. I mean, some of these people could hardly pay for their prescription. They're sitting there going, 'Okay, I have to decide on food on the table or my prescription this month.' And we're trying to sell them something else, like, 'Oh, we're having a special on foot deodorant.'"

AARP officials emphasize that the AARP Pharmacy Service is a "separate" nonprofit organization, which is technically true. The real corporate name of the pharmacy service is "Retired Persons Services, Incorporated," or RPS. Pharmacy leaders downplay the RPS nomenclature for two reasons: they can't survive without the AARP endorsement, and "retired persons services" doesn't spell out their chief purpose—pharmaceuticals. "It isn't a good explanatory name," says McHugh. "We get calls from retired people who hear about it to find out what 'services' we provide."

The explanatory box on its catalogues and other materials says: "Retired Persons Services, Inc., which administers the AARP Pharmacy Service, is a separate entity sponsored, but not owned or controlled, by AARP." True to a point. But what exactly constitutes control? The AARP may not give RPS daily marching orders, but RPS acts like the stepchild of an authoritarian AARP father. McHugh suggests this is done primarily for business reasons. Asked why RPS works hand-in-hand with AARP lobbying positions 100 percent of the time, McHugh answered, "If you get most of your business from one client, you don't likely take positions or do things that are not in their best interest. We have supported AARP positions that might have a negative [impact] on RPS. We said, 'We have to, because that's in the interest of AARP's membership, and we have to support that.' We've done that many times over the years."

The primary mechanism for AARP oversight is the RPS board. Half of RPS's eight board members are AARP officials, all of whom can serve concurrently on the AARP board of directors. "We hear financial reports, we listen to complaints, we make recommendations, and we help the director of the pharmacy run his business," said Francisco Carranco, an AARP–RPS board member.[8] Two more seats on the RPS board are the "Pharmacy" and "Gerontology" seats, held by deans or professors of schools of pharmacy and of gerontology.

The AARP's real goal is to take over more of the prescription drug business market by undercutting mom-and-pop pharmacies and driving them out of business.

Only two of the seats are held by paid RPS employees—its president, Brian Frid, and its treasurer. But having two seats hardly gives RPS independent "control" outside the AARP orbit. Insiders confirm that Frid must bow to the constant "consultative advice" given by AARP Executive Director Horace Deets and AARP Membership Division Director Wayne Haefer. Whenever I asked Frid tough financial questions, he referred me to Deets as the only one with authority to provide such information.

The one way in which the AARP and RPS are truly separate is structurally. The AARP operates from its swank Washington, D.C., headquarters; RPS directs its stepchild empire from across the Potomac River, in Alexandria, Virginia. But the money goes only one way—from RPS to the AARP. Under a licensing agreement for the use of the AARP name and access to its members, RPS pays a royalty of 1 percent of its entire gross sales to the AARP. Neither RPS nor the AARP will discuss these amounts, which have never been revealed outside the organization, but knowledgeable sources report that in 1993 RPS made $440 million, and turned a few tidy millions over to the AARP.

Obviously, a key reason the AARP wants oversight of RPS is because the pharmacy service is a cash cow for the AARP. It's also a double-whammy to the American taxpayer. AARP royalties are tax free and a straight deduction for RPS. Tax-free for the earner; tax-free to the recipient. RPS is set up as a nonprofit organization, though it pays some federal income taxes. "RPS is nonprofit in the sense that it has no shareholders and its net income may be used only in fulfillment of its nonprofit purpose," one RPS official explained in a letter to an inquiring congressman.[9] Frid reiterated in an interview: "Our nonprofit status is a special status related only to the fact that we do not have distribution of excess revenue or profit to stockholders. There are no stockholders to benefit from that." In other words, the nonprofit status is chiefly useful because, instead of sharing profits with stockholders, all of the money is divvied exclusively between RPS and AARP.

The AARP Pharmacy Service has about 2.5 million customers. That's a hefty number, but it's only 8 percent of the AARP's membership. The AARP is quietly expanding that number by engineering a deal with the pharmacy service's traditional enemies—the pharmaceutical firms.

Through surveys, the AARP found that many members just don't want to buy prescriptions from a mail-order company. So the question was: How do we "serve" them (read: get a piece of the action). Answer: through the local pharmacy. Result: a new program still in the testing phase. "RPS President Brian Frid briefed the committee on a new partnership that RPS is forming with a company known as PCS (Pharmaceutical Card System), which is the largest and most successful prescription benefits management company in the country," say the minutes of a March 1994 AARP board meeting. "This is a large market area that the AARP pharmacy has previously been unable to service. The new partnership will benefit current users of AARP's pharmacy by increasing the sales volume and thus lowering total operating costs."

The wording is a bit of public relations flimflam. The reality is less altruistic. It is simply a way for the AARP to get a percentage of retail pharmacy sales. The program, called "Member Choice," provides a discount card to be used at cooperating pharmacies in return for a

$10 annual fee in addition to the $8 AARP membership. For that fee, the program is supposed to guarantee that Member Choice customers will get either at least $1 or 2 percent off the customary price of a prescription at selected pharmacies.[10] AARP has been test-marketing the concept in North Carolina, Colorado, and Alabama, where several major chains like K-Mart, Payless Drug Stores, and Safeway have signed contracts with RPS to participate. The initial results have been encouraging, according to confidential AARP reports. Of the 8,235 membership accounts sold by February 1996, only 1,220 (14.8 percent) were previous RPS customers. The vast majority were "new" members who, though still preferring retail pharmacies, were now filling a quarter of their prescriptions through mail order.[11]

When the AARP first negotiated with PCS to arrange the Member Choice program, PCS was an independent, Arizona-based company. But in July 1994, in a move that alarmed health industry analysts, PCS was bought for $4 billion by the Indianapolis-based pharmaceutical giant, Eli Lilly and Company. An array of pharmaceutical experts said PCS would inevitably have to favor drugs made by its new owner.

Elderly Americans have long been squeezed by pharmaceutical prices that have gone out of sight—and AARP's new partner, Eli Lilly, is one of the firms responsible for this. From 1985 to 1994, prescription drug prices soared almost 100 percent, which was roughly two-and-a-half times as fast as the overall Consumer Price Index. Many individual drugs rose even higher: the price of Premarin, an estrogen-replacement drug that is the most-sold prescription by the AARP Pharmacy Service, jumped 131 percent in just a five-year period, from 1985 to 1990, according to a U.S. Senate report.

Hefty drug price inflation imposes a real human cost as well. "I feel like they rob me without a gun," said seventy-nine-year-old Jo Harris, a Montana widow whose arthritis pills jumped 50 percent in price over two years.[12] Joseph and Margaret Landin of Dallas spend more than $600 of their $1,100 monthly income from Social Security for ten prescription drugs. As drug prices kept rising, they stopped eating out, canceled their newspaper subscription, and decided not to use the air conditioning—even when the Texas heat reached a hundred degrees.[13] "People come in here and actually break down because they can't afford to buy prescriptions," a pharmacist in Greenville, Connecticut, informed President Clinton when he visited the pharmacy. Overall, the AARP estimates that about 10 percent of the elderly have to cut back on necessary items, such as food and heating fuel, to afford their medications.

No single factor has been as effective in reducing drug costs as generic drugs. On this score, the AARP does deserve credit. It has helped to make generic drugs widely available, much to the chagrin of other big pharmaceutical firms. "We certainly haven't always been their favorite son because of our support of generic drugs," brags AARP Pharmacy Service Manager Brian Frid. Along the way, they have countered a brand-name scare campaign aimed at convincing the public that generics don't really work as well as the more expensive medications.

When the AARP Pharmacy Service was founded, most states had laws that prohibited pharmacists from substituting less-costly generic drugs for brand-name products. Working state by state over a decade, AARP lobbyists and volunteers have succeeded in overturning the antisubstitution laws.

BUT NOT ALL of the AARP's lobbying battles on behalf of its pharmacy service customers have been so noble. In fact, the AARP's real goal is to take over more of the prescription drug business market by undercutting mom-and-pop pharmacies and driving them out of business.

"How can I compete with the AARP pharmacy if they are starting out with a much lower cost base?" asked Peter J. Tyczkowsi, chief pharmacist of Pelton's Pharmacy, Middletown, Connecticut, one of the nation's oldest drugstores. "They can charge 10 percent less right off the bat and put other pharmacies out of business."[14]

Inevitably, then, the loyal opposition to AARP's most radical pharmacy positions is the National Association of Retail Druggists (NARD), which represents its thirty thousand independent retail pharmacy members in Washington, D.C. "Look," says NARD spokesman John Rector, "what they do on the pharmacy front is this: they take a position that diverts sales and sometimes ruins your local pharmacist, someone who is offering service, convenience, sales taxes, charitable contributions—investments in the community."[15] Richard Lauring couldn't agree more. He owns a pharmacy in Truman, Minnesota, and was furious when AARP asked him to join it. "I did not join for one reason: they run a mail order pharmacy in competition with my small rural drug store," he said, and added, "Naturally, if someone is acutely ill, they come to me for prescriptions, and then buy all the rest from AARP later."

Generally, competition between businesses is good for the consumer, but some of the community pharmacists' concerns about the AARP are valid. The main ones fall into the following categories:

The AARP eliminates the pharmacist from the safety equation. "My concern is that AARP takes the pharmacist out of the loop," says William Simonson, professor at Oregon State University's School of Pharmacy.[16] "When you act as if going out to buy a bag of pills is like buying a bag of candy, that's potentially jeopardizing the patient. Any time something is boiled down to mail order, there is a potential danger that it could be just product-oriented, instead of a health care service."

AARP gets the profits; local pharmacists get the problems. A vice president with Rite Aid Corp., James Krahulec, told a meeting of the American Pharmaceutical Association that mail service seemed to be skimming "the profit cream" off community pharmacies by capturing the high-volume maintenance drug market "while leaving the high-cost real care of the patient to the local pharmacy."[17] Pharmacists have been known to open doors in the middle of the night because prescriptions hadn't arrived in the mail in time for desperate customers of the AARP and other mail order services.

Some customers call their local pharmacist for instructions on how to take prescriptions they have bought from an AARP pharmacy. "I get a lot of phone calls from their [mail-order] customers on how to take their prescriptions," one independent pharmacist groused to *Drug Topics* magazine.[18] "I tell them, 'You call your [AARP or other mail-order] pharmacist. I don't give out free advice except to my customers.'"

Others bring their AARP/mail-order prescription bottles to local pharmacists to make sure the drugs are still fresh if they change color or show some other irregularity, testified James H. McMahon, an Oak Ridge, Tennessee, pharmacist, before a congressional subcommittee. "So you end up counseling your competitor's customers?" Senator Jim Sasser pressed. "Absolutely," said McMahon. "Retail pharmacy is doing all the consultation work for the mail order pharmacy."[19]

The AARP has lower prices because it doesn't pay property or sales taxes as do the local pharmacists. Property taxes, which can be hefty, add to the cost of operating a retail drugstore. The AARP pays only such taxes for its few warehouses. On the other hand, the AARP Pharmacy Service is supposed to pay state taxes. But in reality, AARP frequently avoids paying the taxes that every other business has to pay.

The AARP argues that prescription drugs are usually exempt from sales tax anyway. True, but over-the-counter drugs and health and beauty aids sold by pharmacies—and the AARP—are generally not exempt. The AARP Pharmacy Services' own internal figures show that 40 percent of their business is made up of these taxable items.

"AARP is not collecting the tax that's due on all those sales," charges Rector of NARD. "There was a Supreme Court decision that left it unclear as to whether states have the authority to require mail-order retailers to collect the tax. So, with this de facto tax exemption, AARP has a built-in 3- to 9-percent sales tax advantage over the local pharmacist's price in any state."

The AARP Pharmacy is unregulated by the states, while local pharmacies must comply with state Board of Pharmacy rules. It makes sense that if a mail-order pharmacy dispenses drugs in a state, it ought to be licensed for that health-care practice. Drugs are potentially dangerous and health-threatening commodities, and should be carefully monitored.

Incredibly, the AARP, the organization that normally loves government regulation on anything that affects the health and well-being of the elderly, is against state regulations requiring a license for its pharmacy service. "States should expand access to competing pharmaceutical suppliers by opposing license laws and regulations that would impose unnecessary and costly burdens on out-of-state, mail-service pharmacy operations," reads the official AARP position.[20] If ever there were a case of the supposedly altruistic AARP lobbying for personal business breaks, this is it.

Some states, like Louisiana and Arkansas, have enacted laws requiring licensing, and the AARP has gone to the Federal Trade Commission, whining about the unconstitutional "restraint of trade." Former secretary of the Arkansas pharmacy board Lester Hosto charged that "the main reason they [mail-order pharmacies] don't want to be licensed is that they don't want that close accountability in each state."[21]

The AARP pharmacy is susceptible to prescription drug fraud. Not surprisingly, it may be easier to get a fake prescription filled by mail than over the counter. In the early 1970s the federal Bureau of Narcotics and Dangerous Drugs (BNDD, the predecessor to the Drug Enforcement Administration [DEA]) found that criminals could obtain a fraudulent prescription from the AARP Pharmacy Service and other mail-order companies one out of four times. On occasion, law enforcement agencies would set up "stings" against the AARP Pharmacy Service, but the AARP caught most of them, McHugh maintains.

The AARP pharmacy makes errors in filling the prescriptions. United States congressional and courtroom testimony is full of examples of patients who received the wrong prescription from mail-order pharmacies. In some of the most extreme cases, the individual died. But these extreme cases have involved mail-order competitors of the AARP, never the AARP pharmacy itself.

Still, NARD says, it's just a matter of time before these discrepancies are uncovered and publicized. They believe any high-volume mail order pharmacy like the AARP must make hundreds, if not thousands, of mistakes.

Finally, government officials favor the AARP Pharmacy Service and other mail-order providers over community pharmacists. It's that AARP halo again. The nonprofit AARP has such a following among government bureaucrats that they promote the AARP pharmacy as if it were not a commercial venture. One example: In a stock response the Food and Drug Administration (FDA) sent in late 1989 to letter-writers concerned about the cost of drugs, the FDA named only the AARP Pharmacy Service as a source of "reduced prices on prescription and nonprescription drugs"—and helpfully provided the AARP's address. Ironically, if the letter-writer wanted to complain, he was advised to write the National Association of Retail Druggists (NARD), address also helpfully provided.

This infuriated NARD's John Rector, who mounted a year-long campaign to get the FDA to halt the selective recommendation. One letter he wrote to FDA Commissioner David A. Kessler in 1991 eloquently spells out the local pharmacists' grievances:

> You can understand our concern when the FDA recommends to consumers who complain about the cost of prescription drugs that they do business with one of our major competitors, the nonprofit AARP....
>
> I am sure you can understand the frustration that these small business persons [community pharmacists] experience when nonprofit entities, serving virtually no charitable interest, compete with them in their marketplace.
>
> You can understand their concern with these competitors that pay no taxes on the income derived from such competition....
>
> I am sure that you can understand the outrage of our members and likely the public at large, when they learn that a federal agency,

supported by their tax dollars, is steering consumers away from local neighborhood pharmacies to a distant "nonprofit" mail order firm which does not abide by the consumer protection statutes....

Even a contemporary Rip Van Winkle would be aware of the special risks and unique threats posed for consumers who utilize mail order pharmacy. Consumers generally do not select mail order pharmacy unless they are coerced to obtain their prescriptions, under insurance contracts, from these unregulated, substandard pharmacies.

To our knowledge, no other country in the world permits pharmacy to be practiced through the mail. Make no doubt about it, the conduct involved is the practice of pharmacy... at the lowest conceivable denominator.

[It] is our expectation that the FDA will no longer take sides in consumer decision-making about the selection of an appropriate pharmacy.... They should be free of the persuasiveness traditionally associated with your hallmark: "FDA approved."[22]

WHEN IT STARTED its mail-order pharmacy program, the AARP promised "savings to our members will be at least 25 percent." Those days are long since gone. San Francisco resident Lynn Pond made a careful comparison between the AARP pharmacy and her favorite local pharmacist.[23] She found the AARP was only "slightly lower, but not so much lower that I am willing to forgo the convenience of a local pharmacy." There is virtually no single drug AARP sells that cannot be obtained cheaper from the neighborhood pharmacy, a discount drug chain, or another mail-order service. When *Money* magazine looked at fifteen drugs commonly used by seniors, the mail-order service of the National Council of Senior Citizens offered consistently lower prices than did the AARP.

I can also report that I received a flood of mail from skeptical AARP members living in more than half of the United States, complaining about the AARP pharmacy. The overall message was caveat emptor. "We can get our prescription medicine $5 to $6 cheaper from Walgreens," wrote Luther and Helen Marcantel of Sulphur, Louisiana. "Their highly touted pharmaceutical program is inferior to many others," says Harvey Gillette of Bella Vista, Arkansas. And from Awbrey Norris of Winter Springs, Florida: "Anyone with the ability to make a meaningful comparison of the mail pharmacy program can do better by not using an AARP service. Discounts? NOT!" A Key West, Florida, resident found that "the prices AARP charges are higher than local pharmacies. What a scam!" Equally irate was Frank Dickman of Manteca, California: "Their so-called savings in health drugs is a fraud. I found prices lower at my local drug store."

The members misunderstand, AARP officials say soothingly. They never promised universal savings, just "reasonable" prices— that is, a "good" service if you can wait a week for your drugs.

But the lack of across-the-board savings is curious, to put it mildly. The AARP Pharmacy Service has every advantage over a local pharmacy: no local property and sales taxes, lower overhead, the ability to buy drugs cheaper with its eight-million-prescriptions-a-year volume—and the nonprofit principle that everything should be sold at a margin sufficient only to cover costs.

So why are the AARP's prices not consistently lower than those of retail pharmacies? The question is so frequently asked by AARP members that the AARP has a stock answer: "In some local areas, drugs frequently taken by older persons have been coming down in price. Some items, including prescriptions, are offered as 'loss leaders.' These are items sold at or below cost to gain a new customer. This means some pharmacies are willing to lose money on prescriptions to attract customers in the hope they will purchase other high profit items."[24] An AARP pharmacy official, reiterating this point, stressed that the pharmacy has "national prices" which can be beaten here or there, but otherwise are "the lowest price you can find in probably 90 percent of the country."

But the evidence indicates that the AARP's prices can be beaten virtually every time, though not always by the local pharmacist.

So forget discount prices, one AARP pharmacy official suggests. "Our real value is service. AARP members like the service." Really? Queried in a confidential survey, customers ranked their satisfaction with the service no higher than their local retail pharmacy.

A confidential AARP survey shows that the median age of an AARP member is 66 years. But the age of the average AARP pharmacy customer is 73.6 years. The median annual income of an AARP member is $30,810. But the average AARP pharmacy customer's annual income is $21,500.[25] One pharmacy official told me that wealthier members didn't use the service because they didn't need to pinch pennies. But another told me that the AARP pharmacy customers were poorer, less-educated, and didn't know there were better deals elsewhere. AARP lobbying chief John Rother is defensive about this. The service is "a good deal for poor people," he insists. "We have a lot of poor people as members of this organization. They save more from the prescription drugs than the $8 membership."[26]

When it started its mail-order pharmacy program, the AARP promised "savings to our members will be at least 25 percent." Those days are long since gone.

Still if AARP were truly charitable, the first thing it would tell all pharmacy customers is that they can save $8 a year right off the top. How? By dropping their AARP membership. You don't have to belong to the AARP to use the pharmacy service. Indeed the RPS is obligated by law to serve all customers. Yet most customers think they have to be an AARP member to use it. James Tabor of Naples, Maine, says he joined the AARP "primarily to take advantage of their discount drug prices." Beatrice Taylor of Hazleton, West Virginia, also joined AARP "hoping to cut down on my drug bill." John Jacobs of Royal, Arkansas, doesn't like the AARP lobby. "AARP does not speak for me on any issue," he says, and the "only" reason he is a member is "for the purpose of purchasing pharmaceuticals." Well, guess what? Save your money and your conscience, James, Beatrice, and John. Drop the AARP membership, and you can continue to buy their drugs.

But don't expect anyone at AARP to volunteer that information.

CHAPTER 9

Pill Pushing

Just because you can buy it through AARP does not mean it's good for you.

—*New York Times columnist Jane Brody*[1]

I understand AARP wants the government to fund medications. Since my husband, a disabled veteran, gets medications through the Veterans Administration, our experience tells us that if seniors ever get government-funded medicine, they will live to regret it. We say, Seniors, beware!

—*Dorothy Willis, Watson, Illinois*[2]

T he AARP has backed every bill that has proposed expanding Medicare to include drug coverage for more than two decades. Needless to say, such legislation would expand the AARP's pill-pushing profits.

Prima facie evidence that AARP officials are looking out for their own interests comes from a confidential 1994 AARP study of members' correspondence.[3] The members' top issue was health care reform. They sent 133,788 letters to AARP headquarters on the subject. Of that total, however, only 152 made reference to "Prescription Drug Coverage"—just *one-thousandth of 1 percent* of the total health care reform letters. Not exactly a hot button issue. Indeed, AARP received four times more letters (665) on gun control—hardly a searing issue for older Americans—than they did on prescription drug coverage. And some, if not the majority, of the letters on drug coverage were actually *opposed* to AARP's love affair with coverage.

"With your help, we're going to get health care right," president Clinton urged AARP members in a videotaped message on the first day of their biennial conference in Anaheim, California, in 1994. "We're going to cover prescription drugs!" On the second conference day, two Clinton cheerleaders drove the point home. Under the president's plan, Assistant Secretary of Aging Fernando Torres-Gil promised, "Eighty percent of your prescription costs will be covered... so you don't have to worry about using your savings or selling your home, or taking food from others or yourselves in order to pay for them." The administration's Bruce Vladeck was just as emphatic. "We need a prescription drug benefit as a central part of the Medicare program—and we need it right away," he said to the sound of scattered applause. "It's time we filled that very central hole in the program. All the folks who don't want to improve or expand programs for seniors have their knives out relative to prescription drugs. I think you know that the President and the First Lady and certainly everyone in the Department of Health and Human Services are very strongly committed to seeing that we get the drug benefit in health care reform. But it's going to be a heck of a fight, and we're going to need a lot of help." The two senior officials and the president were careful not to mention financing the new benefit through Medicare cuts, a subject that would have blown down the whole house of cards.

In the end, AARP officials didn't endorse the Clinton plan, but signed on to a related proposal by Senate Majority Leader George Mitchell (D-Maine), in August. The last-ditch health care reform bill had abandoned the supposedly inflexible Clinton/AARP promise to provide health insurance for *every* American. The Mitchell bill, on the other hand, did include prescription drug coverage for seniors. And there was a suspicious provision tucked away in the 1,443-page bill that would specifically benefit the AARP Pharmacy Service—a clause that largely exempted mail-order pharmaceutical firms from the stringent cost controls that would be imposed on non–mail-order firms. Moreover, according to the Mitchell bill, the government would rebate seniors 25 percent of any extra costs they might incur by using mail-order pharmacy services like AARP's. Unquestionably, as Senator Don Nickles (R-Oklahoma) charged on the Senate floor, "mail-order pharmacies would be given special treatment under this bill."

AARP Executive Director Horace Deets denied any suggestion that revenue enhancing was behind AARP's endorsement. "We had no hand in the crafting of the mail-order prescription drug provision in the Mitchell bill."[4]

Whether the AARP was behind the provision or not, one thing is certain: the AARP doesn't deserve special treatment. The drug coverage it sells in its group health insurance policies is no better than others sold by presumably less-charitable, for-profit companies.

Just ask Betty Fowler of Modesto, California. After turning sixty-five, she applied for coverage under the AARP Group Health Insurance Program. An honest woman, she told them she spent $184 a month on prescription drugs, and would like to buy the AARP plan that included drug coverage.[5] But the AARP spurned Betty Fowler and others like her. "In our efforts to keep our rates reasonable for the entire group, it is necessary for us to medically underwrite the standardized plans containing prescription drug benefits," a form letter informed her.[6] "After careful consideration of your application we cannot enroll you in the plan you selected. Our decision was based on your current drug expenses."

Fowler was properly incensed. "I was shocked at the denial and the statement 'to keep our rates reasonable.' My former insurance carrier—with only several thousand subscribers—covered my drugs with only a $5 to $10 copayment on my part. And AARP—with *millions* of subscribers—cannot do the same? Maybe national health care is not the only thing needing reform. I think reform is in order for AARP."

OLDER AMERICANS HAVE a serious drug problem. Yes, prescription drugs are prolonging and saving lives everywhere, but they can often be more pernicious than palliative. And the AARP knows this. A retired Austin, Texas, physician and AARP board member, John Lione, has testified before the House Subcommittee on Health about it. "The association is deeply concerned about the adverse reactions that can result from mismedication, including drug-induced illnesses, hospitalization, and even death," he said.[7]

The problem is enormous. Occasionally, it has been highlighted when someone famous is afflicted—like the prescription drug addiction of First Lady Betty Ford, or the prescription drug over-dose death of Elvis Presley. But it is bigger than this. It is "so wide-spread that [it is] the nation's *other* drug problem," warned Bryant Welch, executive director of professional practice at the American Psychological Association.[8] As many as 10 percent of all hospital admissions in America can be attributed to adverse drug reactions caused by mismedication.[9] The greatest portion of that number are the elderly, who are not safe from harm even in the hospital itself. Mismedication is often administered to older people when they are hospitalized. No one knows the full dimension of the problem because reporting adverse drug reactions is a *voluntary* program administered as "MEDWatch" by the Food and Drug Administration (FDA). But the state of Rhode Island, for one, found that only about 1 percent of all adverse drug reactions were being reported to the FDA.

One measure of the scope of the problem can be extrapolated from the simple fact that twice as many people in America die from prescription drugs as from illegal narcotics like cocaine and heroin. Of all drug-related deaths, experts have found 70 percent involve prescription drugs.[10] And of these prescription drug-related deaths, at least half were individuals over sixty years old.

According to the National Center for Health Statistics, the chances that a visit to a doctor will result in a prescription for medication is three in five.[11] "Patients too often see doctors as 'drug givers' and themselves as 'drug receivers,'" says Sidney Wolfe, director of the Public Citizen Health Research Group.[12]

A second factor behind adverse drug reactions, besides overprescribing doctors, is that these doctors often fail to ask for—or patients to volunteer—a list of what other medications they are taking. Mixing drugs is dangerous, and sometimes lethal. The elderly, particularly, take a baffling array of prescriptions whose side effects intermix. Senator Claude Pepper often shook his head in disbelief as senior citizens arrived at health subcommittee hearings with large plastic bags filled with pills of every variety. "These were medications that had been prescribed for them, and which they were supposedly taking simultaneously," he recounted. William Simonson, professor at Oregon State University's College of Pharmacy, recalled the case of one older woman admitted to a hospital for "drugged behavior." Indeed. She was taking seventy-five different prescription and non-prescription medications.[13]

Another factor prevalent among the elderly is the tendency to stockpile and swap drugs. This problem is accentuated by mail-order pharmacy services like AARP's, because its customers buy in big volumes. Out-of-date drugs can be harmful. At the least, the dosage may have been so weakened over time that the patient gets worse while falsely believing he should be getting better.

Trading drugs can be even worse. It's not unusual, given the expense of medication, for a husband to use a wife's left-over arthritis drug because it worked for her—without consulting a doctor. Nor is it unusual for seniors to swap drugs with friends and neighbors. One AARP survey found that 10 percent of the elderly respondents said they loaned their prescribed medicines to others, and 7 percent confessed they had "sometimes" borrowed medicine from friends.[14] "The children of the Depression hoard and loan," explains Dr. Ron Anderson, chief of Dallas's Parkland Memorial Hospital. "When I was a pharmacist, I remember [a woman] coming in asking me for 'the blue pill that worked so great for Mildred.' And the day after, I was searching the files to find that blue pill, and she'd say, 'No, no, I think it was red. It definitely was red. It was much better—it was a red pill. Maybe it wasn't Mildred. It might have been Margaret.'"

Another largely unrecognized cause of adverse drug reactions are items as innocent as vitamins. Sometimes, the elderly assume that if you can buy it without a prescription, it must be harmless. "Just because a little bit of something is good for you doesn't mean more is better," warns Jane Brody, health columnist for *The New York Times.* Brody says that "vitamin abuse is rampant among the elderly, and it may be causing more problems than people realize. For example, megadoses of Vitamin C can cause diarrhea and kidney stones, and may interfere with the absorption of B-12 and cause senility. Excessive amounts of Vitamin A can cause loss of appetite, scaly, dry skin, loss of calcium from your bones, and increased pressure in the brain that feels like a tumor. Too much Vitamin D can result in calcium deposits in the kidneys, and block the absorption of Vitamin K. While there is nothing wrong with taking a one-a-day vitamin or mineral supplement, megadoses are largely a waste and may cause health problems. Unfortunately, too many people depend on supplements to make up for a haphazard diet. No pill, or combination of pills can substitute for consuming the right foods."[15]

THE EVILS OF MISMEDICATION can sometimes be traced right back to the source: the drug manufacturer.

Nothing illustrates this better than the Oraflex tragedy of 1982—which conversely turned out to be a moment of justifiable pride for the AARP. The new arthritis drug had been selling in Great Britain for two years before the FDA approved it for sale in the United States in April. Believing it would be a big seller, the manufacturer, Eli Lilly and Company, hyped the drug with a $12 million media blitz. Within six weeks of hitting the market in May, more than 500,000 arthritis sufferers were buying the once-a-day Oraflex.

Adverse drug reactions soon began to appear in the users. The AARP found that eight deaths might be linked to Oraflex use, and perhaps forty-five in Great Britain. The hazard appeared to be the toxic levels of the active ingredient, benoxaprofen, which were building up in the elderly and not being flushed out effectively by their kidneys. The AARP pharmacy chief reported that benoxaprofen remained in the bodies of eighty-two-year-olds nearly four times longer than in persons in their forties. Concerned about this, Eli Lilly asked physicians in June to reduce the standard dosage given to the elderly. They sent out letters to doctors warning of possible liver and kidney damage.

The AARP didn't think this was enough, and elected to take extraordinary action which, in retrospect, probably saved lives. On July 30 AARP wrote the secretary of health and human services, urging a ban on the drug as an "imminent hazard to the lives and health of all Americans, particularly the elderly." Concurrently, the pharmacy service pulled all Oraflex prescriptions from its files and warned patients and doctors about the possible hazards.

Within days, Eli Lilly voluntarily suspended sale of the drug in the United States and Great Britain. John McHugh, the AARP's eminent pharmacist and entrepreneur, feels to this day that the AARP's "actions persuaded Lilly to withdraw their drug." (Oraflex was later reissued in safer, FDA-approved form.)[16]

In the wake of the Oraflex episode, consumer advocates and others began focusing on the testing procedure and found there was a test bias toward younger patients, even though one-third of all prescription drugs are sold to the elderly. One reason was cost. Most animal tests, *Forbes* magazine found, were performed on young, sixty-day-old rats, whose metabolism resembles younger humans. The rats cost $6.82 each; twenty-four-month-old rats, approximating senior citizen human metabolism, cost $72.82 apiece. When testing products on humans, few drug companies did so on people over sixty.[17]

The FDA has instituted some procedures that change the bias of testing and usage on younger adults, but some experts don't think it's enough. Peter Lamy, M.D., chairman of geriatric pharmacotherapy at the University of Maryland School of Pharmacy in Baltimore, reported: "Most of the time we prescribe based on data obtained with younger people, and we extrapolate to all adults."[18] AARP board member John Lione, a physician, testified before Congress:

Many of the drugs used to treat conditions common among the elderly were not clinically tested on older persons. As a result, many drugs do not have specified dosage schedules that are appropriate for elderly patients, and the practitioner is only advised to 'use with caution in elderly or debilitated patients' [which] is not an adequate substitute for clinically-tested safe dosage schedules.[19]

PHYSICIANS AND PHARMACISTS ARE INVARIABLY, and perhaps understandably, more alert to life-threatening adverse drug reactions than to less-severe side effects—and the AARP Pharmacy Service is no different.

"I find it interesting," says Professor William Simonson, "that elderly patients may often be placed on antihypertensive drugs, antidepressants, or antipsychotic medications, all of which may result in sexual impotence, without any attention being given to the possibility that this inhibitory effect on sexual performance may be unacceptable to the patient. Perhaps in the case of elderly patients it is often assumed that their drug-induced sexual impotence will not be noticed!" Yet the opposite is true. Approximately half of individuals over sixty-five engage in coitus regularly, according to major studies, and inability to do so can lead to severe depression.

More widespread ill effects among the elderly are reported for mood-altering drugs. For years after its release in 1963, the most-prescribed drug in the world was Valium, the tiny yellow pill of tranquility. Nursing homes queued up to buy it. In fact, one early three-page ad by the manufacturer was aimed specifically at nursing homes. The ad told how Valium made an old person a "less complaining, less demanding, more cooperative patient." The ad suggested the Valium dosage be "increased gradually as needed and tolerated."[20] The intent was to make life easier for the nursing homes, not keeping the residents active and alert. It became such a scandal that the practice was finally discontinued. That's when researchers noted other hazards of antidepressants—for instance, that they tended to increase the number of injuries seniors had due to falls. A landmark study found that when residents of nursing homes had their antidepressants decreased by 30 percent, the number of falling accidents in those nursing homes decreased by a similar percentage.

A succession of drugs that act on receptors in the brain have been found to have more pronounced effects on the elderly, including addiction, than on the young. A series of "scares" regarding Librium, Darvon, Prozac, and others have been headlined over the years.

The most important study, which entailed six thousand people, was published in the *Journal of the American Medication Association* (JAMA) in August 1994. The study, conducted by Harvard Medical School researchers, found that *one in four* Americans over sixty-five was using prescriptions that were inappropriate or potentially dangerous. In an accompanying *JAMA* editorial, Dr. Jerry Gurwitz observed that the study probably understated the risks experienced by "this vulnerable population." The Harvard researchers used a list of twenty medications that the elderly should rarely take because some don't work or have harmful side effects. The list included sedatives like Valium and Librium, pain relievers like Darvon and Darvocet, and the blood thinner Percantine.[21]

The AARP Pharmacy Service sells all these drugs—and others that pose serious risks to the elderly. As an example, the most widely prescribed drug by AARP, Premarin, is a brand-name yellow .625 milligram estrogen-replacement drug generally bought by women. The loss of the hormone in menopausal and post-menopausal women prompts a host of aggravating ailments like hot flashes and osteoporosis, the loss of bone mass that can cripple. Premarin was designed to ease that suffering, and has since been found to offer women some protection against cardiovascular disease.

But, for all those potentially wonderful benefits, the hormone-replacement therapy carries a significant cancer risk: Studies have found that there is a sixfold increase in uterine cancer among women taking estrogen, and a fourfold increase in breast cancer when taken with progesterone.[22]

THESE SORTS OF SIDE EFFECTS and drug interactions underline that the undoing of the AARP Pharmacy Service is the possibility of mismedication.

Good pharmacists are desperately needed to backstop mistakes prescribing doctors may have made. Common sense says a local pharmacist who knows his customers is more likely to discern possible adverse drug reactions than an AARP telemarketer. Even if AARP mails drugs with "Medication Information Leaflets for Seniors," the community pharmacist knows his customers, he can ask relevant questions, and he can make sure a patient knows how and when to take his prescription drug.

If the AARP had its way, and seniors could use the AARP's mail-order pharmacy to get drugs for free (paid for by Medicare), what would be the result? A senior official at the AARP Pharmacy Service, walking through the logic of the case, conceded—off the record—that "if it's going to cost less for drugs, or cost nothing, then the consumption is going to be a lot higher." And, he agreed, overmedication problems would explode. The billions of dollars spent on hospitalizing seniors who used their medications improperly might double or triple. Prescription drug abuse, addiction, and drug-related deaths would multiply.

Was there a bright side in this dismal picture?

Yes, he smiled a bit mischievously. Then he paused before leaning forward and adding: "The sales of drugs by the AARP Pharmacy Service would probably go through the roof, if the government allowed patients a choice of providers. And, of course, the royalty we pay AARP would also double or triple!"

CHAPTER 10

Membership: The AARP's Pawns

We're here to make changes for the members where it counts—on the Hill and in state capitals—not to jump in bed with every insurance company and discounter who comes along.

*—AARP staff lobbyist, as cited
in an internal survey*[1]

Those who would politicize AARP's membership on public issues will eventually kill the goose with the golden eggs.

—AARP staffer in the same survey[2]

"Welcome to Wayne's World" flashes the greeting on a blue computer screen when an AARP employee wants to interact with the Membership Division.

The division is the biggest boy on the AARP block—the power division among the ten—and was long ruled by "Wayne," former Montana teacher Wayne Haefer.[3] Membership is where the money is. Income from all the products and services that the AARP hawks comes through the "Member Services" department of the Membership Division. The only significant revenue the division doesn't handle is advertising income from AARP publications.

"Yes," agrees John Rother, director of the legislative division, "*that's* the empire."[4]

At one 1995 senior AARP staff meeting, Wayne Haefer subtly underlined the point of conflict between its lobbying and business divisions. He reported the results of one of the AARP's most confidential surveys. It showed that 86 percent of the AARP's members did not cite lobbying representation as their primary reason for joining the organization.[5] Many of the 14 percent who said they *were* interested in "representation" either weren't sure what the AARP's lobbying positions were or were opposed to them. In short, as Haefer pointed out, membership declines when the AARP takes a strong position on the Hill.

He then carefully outlined why positions like endorsing big-spending health care reform bills were counterproductive. The more members know about AARP positions, the more disagreements and resignations. And declining membership means less power on Capitol Hill.

When lobbyist Rother was asked whether senior AARP officials had ever proposed his division's demise, he said, "No one's proposed it to my face, but I'm sure there are *certain people* who would love that."[6]

The AARP's former public relations director, Lloyd Wright, isn't surprised by the AARP's internal conflict. "There have always been those in the legislative office who bend AARP's policy to serve interests other than the elderly, in my judgment. Some of them think the AARP has a responsibility to engage in every issue that comes before Congress of national interest. But I realized that there was only one commonality that defines an AARP member—it's their birthday, fifty years of age or older. That's it."[7]

One of the better internal studies of the AARP was made by New York–based Chester Burger & Company, Incorporated. "This report has been prepared solely for the internal use of the American Association of Retired Persons," the title page orders. "Its contents are restricted to internal distribution"—meaning senior paid staff *only*. One section is worth quoting in full:

Many on the staff... expressed confusion about the diversity of AARP membership demographics. They are uncomfortable with a population that includes the affluent, the needy, retired people, those still working, the mature, the old, the old old, the feeble elderly, active seniors, etc. As membership characteristics become more pronounced, the issues gain complexity.

The question for many: "Who is AARP's constituency, and how does it best serve them?" As a result, we found growing tension over tactics and a deepening rift between two camps: membership growth/service and advocacy on public policy issues.

The service camp says that taking sides and speaking out on issues will polarize members and alienate potential members. They feel the mounting advocacy campaigns will subject AARP to increased criticism, ultimately retard membership growth and curtail the delivery of services to members.

The advocacy faction believes AARP must be outspoken... and lead the national dialogue about issues important to the aging. They fear the low-profile, don't-rock-the-boat attitude of the services [membership growth] camp will prevent them from being heard on key issues. They fear that AARP will be seen as "money-making fat cats."

We encountered some *destructive static*—not healthy tension—between these two opposing views of AARP's mission.[8]

THE MOST BASIC WORK of the Membership Division is recruiting new AARP members.

Ruling this roost is forty-two-year-old Melinda Halpert, director of Membership Development, a twelve-year AARP veteran. Halpert is a no-nonsense, high-powered AARP executive, which makes her something of an exception. Acquiring new members for the AARP is not a job you can fudge; unlike most AARP jobs, its success or failure is wholly quantifiable.

But lately, the results have not been too encouraging. One couple from Geneva, New York, Robert and Norma Lamberson, wrote: "We are not members of AARP, and doubt that we will ever join because we have a very negative impression of them. We are each fifty-seven years old, and every year since we turned fifty we have each received several 'invitations' to join AARP. If all people over fifty are solicited as often as we are, this must be a tremendous expense."[9]

The Lambersons hit the nail on the head. AARP financial documents show Halpert spends at least $8 million each year just on printing and mailing "membership acquisition" solicitations. Including "membership retention" mail, Halpert's shop sends as many as one hundred million pieces of mail out each year, according to AARP sources.[10] That's one hundred times what the average large-sized company would do.[11] Halpert's full budget is around $60 million.

The truth is, without direct mail the AARP would have to fold its tent: During the first six months of 1996, according to AARP confidential reports, direct mail brought in an average of 148,450 new members a month while all other methods brought in 27,157 members per month. But the AARP has been suffering in recent months from a downhill trend in their direct mail response rates.

The AARP's experts reassured the board that "in spite of lower response rates and higher costs," AARP's direct mail results "are very respectable" because of a trend of declining response rates industry wide."[12]

Another and important reason for the shrinking response rates is that the AARP makes millions of mailing mistakes every year that cost millions of dollars. Not only does the AARP solicit an estimated forty thousand individuals a month who are too young to join the AARP, AARP sources estimate the association solicits more than five million people every year who are dead.

Hence the all-time funniest AARP solicitation—Mark Twain. The AARP sent an application to Mr. and Mrs. S. Clemens—Twain's real name—at the Hartford, Connecticut, address of his memorial home.[13] Officials at the memorial thought it would be hilarious to fill out the application and send it back. They identified his birthdate as 1835 and even added the tip-off: "You may know me better by my pen name, Mark Twain." Elaine Cheeseman, education director of the memorial, laughed: "I thought that would give it away." But the AARP machine droned on and returned a medical identification card addressed to Twain, along with a request for his membership fee.

STILL, DEAD MEMBERS are the minority. The average member of the AARP is white, sixty-six years old, has attended or graduated from college, lives in the suburbs, and has an annual income of more than $30,000.

The AARP knows this but doesn't want anyone else to, because each year it conducts a new "Membership Demographics Analysis," a report

> Not only does the AARP solicit an estimated forty thousand individuals a month who are too young to join, the association solicits more than five million people every year who are dead.

whose distribution is so limited that copy numbers are handwritten on each of them. "CONFIDENTIAL" is stamped in boldface across the top, and in a shaded box on the bottom appears: "This report has been prepared for limited distribution to AARP membership staff. It contains confidential information about AARP members. The only data that can be disseminated to the public would be that on age, gender and regional locations."[14]

Interestingly, the three items that the membership staff is allowed to talk about are those in which the AARP membership matches the general fifty-plus population in the United States. For instance, the AARP is 56 percent female, about the same number as the older U.S. population (55 percent). But the rest of the primary indicators—including race, education, and income—are startlingly out of skew with the older U.S. population. Indeed, these confidential surveys show what congressmen and critics have long suspected but were unable to back: that the Americans who belong to the AARP—48 percent of all those over fifty—are whiter, richer, and better-educated than the general older population.

Two percent of the AARP's members are black, 2 percent are Hispanic, and 2 percent are Asian Americans or another minority—

only 6 percent of AARP's total membership comes from minority groups, compared to 13 percent of the general over-fifty population, according to census data.

In AARP lingo, underrepresentation of minorities is not a problem, but an "area of opportunity." This particular opportunity has encouraged the association to advertise in some ethnic magazines and over radio stations geared to a minority audience, but nothing has so far made much headway. "It's much more expensive to recruit ethnic groups than it is just your average population. They perceive AARP as a white organization, so why would they want to join?" explained one AARP marketing expert. Still, most of the staff doesn't think the organization has done enough to recruit minorities. "Diversity issues surfaced any time membership was raised, and in almost every session," notes one confidential survey of staffers.[15]

The AARP is also missing out on a huge number of elderly who live in cities. "AARP appears to be for the more prosperous senior citizen," wrote one older American from San Francisco.[16] "It misses the seniors stuck in the city with street crime rampant and the police looking the other way. We are afraid, alone, and don't know what to do." Less than a third (30 percent) of AARP members live in cities; only 29 percent live in rural areas. The bulk of them—41 percent—live in suburbs (including planned retirement communities).[17]

"We are mostly a suburban organization," observed one of the AARP's membership statisticians. "We are doing little to recruit in the cities, but we are trying to turn things around in the rural areas. We have a pilot project, called the Deep South Project.... The Deep South is our lowest penetration area. They're the poorest, too, which makes them less likely to join. And there's also a cultural thing which came up in the research. Southerners are much more suspicious of big government—which is what they perceive AARP to be, organizationally—than the rest of country is."

One of the more startling indicators that AARP members are significantly more upscale than nonmembers is their educational accomplishments: 52 percent of AARP members have attended or graduated from college as compared to 29 percent of the fifty-plus population, according to the 1994 Membership Demographics Analysis. And higher education usually translates into higher incomes.

This is the critical conflict—the deep pockets of the AARP's elderly who can afford higher taxes versus the majority of the American elderly population who cannot. "It's a very affluent Senior Citizen group—not the average hard-working paycheck-to-paycheck citizen. It's a powerful organization controlled by the Rich & Powerful," writes Francis Ikler of Idaho Falls, Idaho, who says she is no longer a member.

The AARP's members are getting richer every year, as seen in the six confidential demographics analyses from 1989 to 1994.

> 1989: $23,852
> 1990: $24,500 (3 percent increase)
> 1991: $26,200 (6 percent increase)
> 1992: $27,600 (5 percent increase)
> 1993: $28,300 (2 percent increase)
> 1994: $30,810 (8 percent increase)

This measures income only—pensions, interest, Social Security, dividends—not investments, which are often quite large. According to the AARP's own figures, four-fifths of all wealth in the United States is held by Americans over the age of sixty-five.

Scanning the AARP's premiere publication, *Modern Maturity*, cements the impression of AARP affluence. "At sixty-six, I am still able to work and earn a decent living," writes Lois Cherner of San Francisco.[18] "If I ever retire, I could never live the kind of lifestyle AARP's magazine writes about. Those people are rich. Most retired people in this country, especially women, are *not* rich." William Whittaker of Port Ewen, New York, couldn't agree more: "In my mind, they represent the most affluent and privileged interest group in the country—save corporate lobbyists. A look at their advertisers in *Modern Maturity* suggests a target market with lots of discretionary income—hardly a put-upon class."[19]

AARP OFFICIALS LIKE OUTSIDERS to think that the AARP's members join because they're vitally interested in AARP's information, its lobbying, and its volunteer opportunities. They cringe when critics like Alan Simpson suggest members mostly join for the discounts. "People really know about AARP because of the discounts," concedes Richard Henry,[20] the chief executive officer under Horace Deets, though he believes that most people don't actually *join* "for the discounts." Maybe, but Melinda Halpert, the AARP's membership development chief, explained in *Direct*, a trade publication, "our strongest offers have been where we portray a whole buffet of member benefits."[21]

While many bargain-hunting members are only likely to feel cheated—receiving fewer true discounts than they expect—members who join in order to work as volunteers are likely to feel exploited.

IN 1990, AT SIGNIFICANT EXPENSE, the AARP Program Resources Department created, packaged, and distributed a board game called *Volunteer Management* for a group of senior staffers. It was not intended for general distribution, and was kept to a small circle of AARP officials who wrestle with the problem of controlling more than one hundred thousand volunteers. "If some of the volunteers knew about it, they might be offended," confessed one senior official.[22]

But *Volunteer Management* is a game that is neither fun to play nor amusing in its underlying message. The successful formula for the AARP is simple and has a proven two-decade track record: make sure a core group of AARP volunteer leaders across the country have passed a political litmus test, and then use them to control the rest. AARP has found that retired educators and government employees are more likely to agree with their campaign for bigger government. The few cantankerous conservatives or other free-thinkers who slip through this vetting process either eventually succumb to AARP peer pressure, or are voted into a corner and made pariahs.

"Training" is key to the AARP's volunteer manipulation. As Mildred B. McCauley, a member of the board of directors from 1988 to 1994, noted: "I have met so many AARP volunteers who are involved and extremely loyal to the association, but until they have received training from the National (headquarters) by the staff, they had not known the AARP purposes, which they were asked to support."

After attending an annual orientation conference, the volunteer leader is flooded with "information" from AARP headquarters telling him what positions to take on political issues. For instance, even though the majority of the AARP's members were, judging by the volume of phone and letter protests, opposed to socialized healthcare, AARP came out in support of the controversial 1994 Mitchell–Gephardt healthcare plan. Of the AARP's 4,071 volunteer chapter leaders, however, only "a few" warned the grassroots rebellion.

Presidents and congressmen live in fear of the AARP because its lobbyists purport to represent an army of 350,000 volunteers who can make legislators' lives miserable. Because this oft-cited number represents just 1 percent of the AARP membership, it is never questioned.

While many bargain-hunting members are only likely to feel cheated—receiving fewer true discounts than they expect—members who join in order to work as volunteers are likely to feel exploited.

However, in the 1994 "AARP Volunteer Census," an internal AARP document, volunteer figures were shown to have fallen dramatically, from a 1991 high of 384,551 to just 161,974 in 1994.[23] Evidently, AARP had grossly inflated the figures in the past. A top AARP volunteer coordinator was trying to make the figure honest. "People who work with the chapters came to me and said, 'You know, there's really no way we can document those [larger] numbers,'" she recalled.

Yet even the smaller number may be inflated, because it was based not on a head count, but by assuming that every volunteer chapter had at least nineteen active members. My own research indicates this to be wishful thinking.

What congressmen really worry about are committed, politically-minded AARP volunteers. But this is a smaller number still. According to the internal census, the bulk of the volunteers operate nonpolitical AARP programs and chapters. It shows that there are only 2,774 AARP volunteers specifically committed to assisting in lobbying either federal or state governments.

Nevertheless, outside observers, who are less well-informed, continue to perpetuate the myth, providing an unwitting assist to the AARP. "No other volunteer organization—including the Democratic and Republican parties—can marshal so large and unified a force in the field," wrote one author.[24] "It is the permanent field force, not the money, or the small army of lobbyists, or the research and publicity resources of the Washington headquarters, that is the secret of AARP's power." The real truth is that the AARP is a paper tiger.

Savvy congressmen know this. But evidently, House Speaker Newt Gingrich does not. In October 1997 Gingrich bowed to the AARP by considering Horace Deets to serve on a Medicare reform commission. As an October 29, 1997, *Washington Times* article reported, "Gingrich struck a deal with Mr. Deets before the 1996 elections: If the association would lay off Republicans, their director would be named to the Medicare panel." House Majority Leader Dick Armey (R-Texas) described the idea of appointing Deets as "horrible," perhaps especially because President Clinton, Democratic House Minority Leader Dick Gephardt (Missouri), and Democratic Senate Minority Leader Thomas A. Daschle (South Dakota) had their own slots to fill on the panel. Nevertheless, Armey refused to buck Gingrich's choice and Gingrich's alleged deal appears to have paid off with a more quiescent AARP.

Gingrich's intention was to "begin a dialogue with [the AARP]," and "to know where they were coming from," according to one Gingrich staffer. But it appears that Gingrich fears the AARP, perhaps because the association has been so aggressively wooed by President Clinton. Gingrich once admitted to AARP board members, "I want you to know that I can't do what I want to do... without you."

BUT THE FACT IS, several smaller organizations have been able to mount larger write-in and call-in campaigns to Congress. To judge by dedicated member response, the National Rifle Association, the Sierra Club, and at least three other seniors organizations—the National Committee to Preserve Social Security, the Seniors Coalition, and the National Council of Senior Citizens—are far more effective.

Ask any congressman about the largest, most concentrated constituent response of the past decade, and he or she will say it was the repeal of the Medicare Catastrophic Act in 1989. This was a bill the AARP was instrumental in getting passed. But after it was passed, defecting AARP members agitated for repeal. Numerous appeals and "legislative alerts" from AARP leadership failed to activate even a smattering of volunteers to counter this rebellious tide. The loss was so large and devastating for the AARP that the staff realized they could not afford to show such weakness again.

Not all of the AARP's "public policy" volunteer lobbyists are targeted at Washington. Many focus on state governments, where they can have more clout, though still do not always win. For example, within days of losing the national health care reform battle in 1994, the AARP's liberal California state leadership was throwing its resources into California's Proposition 186, a single-payer health care bill. Single-payer means having the government take over the entire health care system, as in Canada. But dissident AARP members again refused to respond, and the measure ultimately failed, despite AARP's support.

Another example of the AARP working against its members' interests is its support of higher taxes, including property taxes, which are particularly burdensome to the elderly, but who can be forced out of their homes because of the inflationary cost of property taxes. AARP mounted an unsuccessful campaign in California's against Proposition 13, the landmark 1978 referendum that limited property taxes to 1 percent in that state. Two years later, AARP lobbying did help defeat Proposition 9, which sought to cut California's income tax in half.

The AARP has fought in state after state against similar property and income tax cuts, and has often succeeded. The AARP has also lobbied for tax increases that obviously strike harder at the elderly who are generally unable to offset the cost by earning more income. But it is not just politics for which volunteers are used; it is generating profits. For example:

> AARP sells a driver's training course for older Americans called "55 Alive." If the members pay the fee and take the course, they are promised a roughly 10 percent discount on their auto insurance. Thanks to successful lobbying, thirty-seven states now require that insurance companies *must* offer this discount to graduates of the AARP program.[25]

THAT IS GOOD FOR SALES of "55 Alive," but whether it is good for auto safety and the insurance rates of other Americans is doubtful. A senior AARP lobbyist admitted to me that "everybody else's insurance rates are up higher since the older people who take the AARP-sold course get a 10 percent discount. And there's no decrease in accidents or anything because the effect of the course wears off in a few weeks, and they're back to less-responsible older habits."

On a state-by-state basis, the AARP fought banking industry curbs on money market funds. Why? Because the AARP derived substantial income from selling those funds. Without seeming to discern a conflict of interest, The *AARP News Bulletin* promoted the fact that some of these bills "sought to prohibit checking convenience offered by many funds, including the AARP U.S. Government Money Market Trust."[26] The money-making arm of the AARP couldn't have that, and the volunteers were mobilized.

THE AARP BYLAWS and handbooks abound with warnings to the chapters about what can happen if they fail to support the AARP's political and business goals. An AARP chapter can be disowned for "recurrent failure to conform to the policies and standards of AARP," and chapter leaders can be removed "with or without cause at any time," according to the handbook. If a chapter wants to take an official position on a local political issue, it must first ask permission, "to ensure their positions are consistent with the Association's goals and legislative policy.... If chapter leaders or members propose an activity or position that conflicts with AARP policy and the difference cannot be resolved, these individuals must not present their positions as representative of the Association or chapter. They also should not denigrate AARP's position."[27]

Savvy congressmen know the AARP is a paper tiger. But evidently, House Speaker Newt Gingrich does not. In October 1997 Gingrich bowed to the AARP.

The AARP policy manual for volunteers warns: "AARP encourages its volunteers and chapters to communicate ideas, opinions, questions, and concerns to appropriate persons within the Association. However, volunteers will not express opposition to AARP's policies or positions to others while performing their volunteer duties or when they might be perceived as representing AARP."[28]

Paul Hewitt of the National Taxpayers Union Foundation notes that it is "curious that with a heterogeneous membership of 34 million... there is none of the robust debate within AARP seen in other large, politically active membership organizations.... This silence is no accident, but is the product of a systematic campaign by AARP's Washington staff to chill debate and dissention within its volunteer ranks."

The AARP has never gone so far as to yank a chapter's charter for rabble-rousing, but a few chapter leaders have found themselves sent out the door with a pat on the back and a nice letter thanking them for their service, which was no longer required. Townsend L. Walker of Huntsville, Alabama, says he was "railroaded" off the board of directors of his chapter because he would not toe the party line. He came away from the experience feeling that "insidious shenanigans at the top have stifled our voice, made robots of the membership, and tarnished the original Andrus vision of a progressive organization of retired people."[29]

Charles Galbraith joined the Waynesboro, Pennsylvania, chapter, and was impressed by the intentions and efforts of the volunteers there. But when he started perusing AARP publications, he concluded the organization was "constantly pushing some big government, socialistic scheme," that didn't fit his own politics. He petitioned Washington for permission to remain a member of the local chapter but drop his national membership. His request was denied.

Chapter leaders complain that there are no serious discussions of AARP policy at the many workshops and conventions where members are superficially invited to give their input. Their suggestions and resolutions sent up to headquarters are ignored unless they conform to positions already decided upon by the national leadership. As former AARP volunteer Henry Gleich of West Hurley, New York explains, "I have a very negative picture of the AARP from the inside. I once believed that change could be initiated from within AARP. I was wrong. Any such effort is ignored and discouraged. For instance, resolutions by local chapters are rejected unless they conform to headquarters staff's preordained policy.[30] Another veteran AARP senior staffer and member of the executive council laments, "Look, for the national staff, when it comes to volunteers, we know we need a hell of a lot of them, and the most important thing to do is manipulate them. The way we manipulate them is to entertain them, pay their expenses, and make sure they never make a single decision." Morton Schaps of Walnut Creek, California, says, "I was a local chapter vice-president for one year and that chapter's president for two years. *Never* during my membership was I or the local chapter solicited for an opinion on any issue. Only when the firestorm on AARP's support for catastrophic health insurance erupted, did a state official attend a chapter meeting to try to explain and justify AARP's position."[31]

Ed Lewis, a former member of AARP's Washington State Legislative Committee, thought it would be a splendid idea if the AARP surveyed its members in his state to see how they felt about the catastrophic care legislation as it was making its way through Congress. The AARP headquarters sent an emissary to Lewis. His survey was corrected and rewritten. "They'd bring out a new draft and say, 'Your draft wasn't right'—literally telling me what I should do." His legislative committee fell apart in the dispute over the survey. Lewis also found that volunteers who stuck to the party line would be invited to training sessions and conventions, where they were wined and dined and booked in top hotels.

Lack of enthusiasm for the chapters at AARP headquarters may stem from the surveys the AARP has taken over the years. Those surveys consistently show that AARP members who join the chapters are older, less well educated, and less likely to be active in other community activities than the typical AARP member who doesn't join a chapter. There are exceptions to the rule, like the chapter in Irving, Texas, that forced the city council to reverse a policy against hiring retirees as school crossing guards.[32] But the exceptions don't add up to enough to make the AARP leadership see the chapters as assets in the AARP political agenda.

Though publicly, Executive Director Horace Deets has talked about building the AARP at the local level, he has little interest in the volunteer chapters. "How do you revitalize something that was never vital in the first place?" he said in a closed-door high-level staff meeting. Chapters are "just pouring money down a rat hole."

But as a nonprofit, tax-exempt organization, isn't the AARP supposed to spend its money on charitable, worthy causes? When Ethel Percy Andrus made her list of the things AARP "Is" and "Is Not," in the "Is Not" column, Andrus wrote that the AARP "does not exploit its members for either political or partisan profit." It does now.

CHAPTER 11

The Grandchildren's Bill

> I can't see how the AARP can keep demanding more when the source of it all, the younger workers, are struggling now.
>
> —*Jim Engler, former AARP member,*
> *Pittsburg, Kansas*[1]

> **Sadly, AARP is willing to mortgage the future of our children and grandchildren, if necessary, to achieve its purpose—the preservation and enhancement of Social Security and Medicare.**
>
> —*Robert L. Osborne, former AARP member,*
> *Lakeview, Arkansas*[2]

At AARP's national convention in San Antonio, Texas, in 1992, Lee Iacocca uttered a warning:

In too many ways, I'm afraid, we're seeing the generations growing apart instead of growing together. And I'm afraid that most of that blame is ours, because we haven't followed the AARP motto, "To serve and not be served." We have not served that younger generation too well.

Rebuffed by silence, the sixty-year-old Iacocca went on:

I tell them about all the important things that our generation did, like winning the Cold War to putting a man on the moon. I talk about some of the diseases we've cured, some of the bullies we've beaten, some of the injustices we've righted. I tell them we're leaving them a world that's a little more secure, a little more humane, and generally a little more decent place to live than when we found it.

And just when they start to feel all warm and wiggly about us, and right when they aren't looking, I hit 'em with a dose of reality: I say, "Oh, yeah, and one more thing: we forgot to pay for all of this. *We're going to let you pick up the check.*" And then it gets a little somber, a little quiet.

It got equally quiet among the AARP attendees. He continued:

I tell them that in addition to their student loans, they've got a $4 trillion national debt on the books. And that happens to come to $16,000 for every last one of them. Every man, woman and child. I tell them they have a $300 billion—think of that—annual interest bill on that to handle, because of the debt. And I tell them that they have to pay that interest bill every year before they can even think about fixing our schools, which are a mess, and rebuilding our roads and bridges, which are crumbling before our eyes, or fixing the ozone hole in the sky that they say could wipe out life on earth some day.

See, I level with them. *I tell them I'm not very proud that my generation is doing this to them. No other generation in history has buried its kids under a dungheap of public debt like we have.*

But I don't tell them the whole truth. I just want to get out of there with my honorary degree and my life. So I skip a few of the ugly details—like the fact [that] an average 30-year-old man today will pay almost $200,000 in taxes more than he will ever receive from Social Security, Medicare, or any government program. But if you're an average 70-year-old man, you've already gotten back in benefits just about all the taxes you ever paid. And before you die, you'll get about $65,000 more in benefits than you'll pay in taxes.

Now this guy has a right to be mad: he's 30 years old. He's trying to buy a house and raise a family. He's been told that his generation will be the first one whose lifestyle won't match their parents. And now, he has to pay the leftover bills for that lifestyle that he's not going to get for himself. And then 30 years from now, when he retires, and all he has are those IOUs, he'll have to tax his own kids at an even larger rate than he was taxed just so he can get that Social Security check each month.

I want to tell you something—I think if I had my choice, I'd rather be starting out as a college graduate in 1946, when I did, instead of graduating from college today, sad to say. Yes, we budgeted, we sacrificed and we were responsible. But then we stood by and let Washington hang a $4 trillion albatross of debt around the necks of our kids. Where did we go wrong?

Not only have the baby boomers been squeezed by the AARP's big-government agenda, but they are culturally divorced from the traditional AARP member.

THE FEW MINUTES OF COLD truth delivered by Chrysler Chairman Lee Iacocca went unapplauded.

The irony is, the AARP needs the next generation, the baby boomers who have been footing the bill, to join the association. Not only have the baby boomers been squeezed by the AARP's big-government agenda, but they are culturally divorced from the traditional AARP member.

"The concept that the boomers are going to now be entering the mature market is hogwash," advises Cheryl Russell, a former editor of *American Demographics* magazine and author of *The Master Trend: How the Baby Boom Is Remaking America*.[3] Baby boomers don't identify with the older generation—nor even with the aging process itself. They won't concede the years. "When thinking about the baby boomers entering their fifties, just forget about marketing to the mature market and think from scratch. The baby boom in every stage of life has rewritten the rules."

THE DIFFERENCE MAY BE TOO GREAT for the AARP to bridge. Already, they haven't been able to bridge the differences between younger and older members. "I fail to see where my 'interests' at age 53 can be anywhere at all the same as my parents aged 82 and 83," wrote Richard Lauring from Truman, Minnesota.[4] By using "focus groups," Sharon Krager, the AARP's Director of Integrated Marketing, discovered that "younger participants (ages 50 to 60) felt that AARP would be a more useful organization when they are older, but that it doesn't offer them very much now."[5] Paul Steen, the top volunteer leader in Minnesota, didn't need a focus group to realize that.[6] "When people between fifty and sixty come into an organization that seems to be dominated by those in their late seventies and eighties, they say, 'What am I doing here?' People tend to stick with their own particular generation."

At least one AARP strategic planning document[7] has conceded the near-impossibility of merging the generations:

> The question of relevance to generations was articulated by the experts [in AARP focus groups] who think that the difference in interests between the 50s age group who are "still connected" and the "average 75-year-old member" was insurmountable. While the "older, more affluent, white member was living on retirement income, enjoying travel and leisure," *Boomers* at the cusp of membership felt they were "hostages in Potomac," trying to pay off mortgages on houses too big for their empty nests, paying college tuitions, and wondering if they will ever be able to retire—and what they would live on if they could!

ONE PARTICULARLY INSIGHTFUL observation came from over-sixty-five AARP Chairman of the Board Robert Shreve:[8] "When I think back at my own life, and my parent's lives—my generation went to its parent's churches, joined the same Kiwanis and Rotary Club, came home from the service and joined the American Legion, or the Veterans of Foreign Wars, or whatever. The generation of my children generally did not do that. They didn't join the same churches—they didn't go to church at all, maybe. Or they didn't join the service clubs. They were much more likely to be joining special interest clubs. They started their own veterans organization after the Vietnam War. *So why would we think, for a minute, that they're going to flock into AARP when they turn eligible?*"

So, predicted one AARP department head: "Membership will continue dropping off because the greatest pressure is on renewals for the younger members. They're going—there's no reason for them to stay because there's nothing here for them."

Not only is there nothing for them at the AARP, but the AARP has left a bad taste in their mouths as a tax-hungry generational villain. The AARP, like Congress, may have taxed itself into disrepute. It appears that the AARP has endangered their retirement and their children's future.

CHAPTER 12

The Secret Decline of the AARP

> I joined AARP at 50. I will not renew because they are not a service organization. For some discounts and a cheap membership, they manage to give the impression they speak for the elderly. False! The membership and the elderly are not some monolithic block. It is a giant lobbying machine, and a fraud.
>
> —*John F. Lescher, Wakefield, Massachusetts*[1]

> AARP made a hell of a lot of money selling insurance and conveying the idea that old age is a time for having fun and taking trips. It's good to see they now have a social conscience.
>
> —*Maggie Kuhn, founder, Gray Panthers*[2]

The AARP's membership is "dropping like a stone," concedes one of their top officials in a confidential interview. But the AARP is determined to keep this quiet. It is so determined to hide this that, in July 1995, they secretly altered the books to give themselves, literally, an overnight boost of more than two million members—without receiving a single new membership application.

To understand what a shock the declining membership numbers are to long-timers, consider the boast that Horace Deets made over breakfast at the Statler Hilton in June 1987. Then chief of staff, Deets was briefing incoming Executive Director Jack Carlson on the organization's first attempts at "strategic planning." According to Carlson's handwritten notes, they were confidently expecting *forty-one million members* "by the 1990s." These days, AARP insiders know, they'll be happy if they can just stay even with about thirty-two million members by the year 2000.

The situation has become so disconcerting internally, that top officials feel they are forced to make a virtue out of necessity. When Deets reports to the board of directors about the numbers, he is not downcast or apologetic. He cheerily tells them everything is going along swimmingly, because his "strategy" of "break-even growth" or "modest growth" is going just as planned. It's a bit like the CEO of a major corporation telling his stockholders that the company experienced only a 1/2 percent profit—just as planned, because why make more money?

No, the truth is unsettling. This is an organization which has averaged nearly one million new members each year since it was founded. But not recently. At the beginning of 1994 the AARP had 33,176,654 members. By the end of the year—which featured the health care reform debacle—they had lost a million members. Since then, instead of gaining a million members a year, they seem to be losing them, and the trend is downward. The baby boomers started turning fifty in 1996. Four million did so by the end of the year. But in the first six months, when the AARP had a new pool of two million potential members, membership dropped by 660,000. It was shaping up to be an even worse year than the previous one.

Outsiders, and most AARP staffers, are unaware of the depth of the membership drop because the AARP hid it with a neat little sleight of hand called the "spouse factor." The AARP has actually never had even twenty-three million members who pay the $8-a-year membership. But the thirty-three-million-member figure has been frequently used because the AARP gives a free membership to the applicant's spouse.[3] So, inside the AARP, when they talk about paid memberships, they refer to it as twenty-two million "households." For more than a decade, they figured that there was one living spouse in every two households. So, using a formula accepted by advertisers in their publications, they multiplied the number of households by 1.5 to come up with a total membership count.

But in a closed-door session in July 1995, the board agreed that, since the numbers were dropping at an embarrassing rate, they would reverse the downward spiral. They would now multiply the number of households by 1.6. The effect, in a single day, was to increase the number of reported members from 31.65 million to 33.76 million. They thus received a paper boost of 2.11 million members in a twenty-four–hour period, and the new number of 33 million was quietly included in the standard last paragraph of all AARP press releases.

Nevertheless, by the summer of 1996, that number shrank to 32.6 million members. Compare the bare numbers to membership in 1993, and that's a fall-off of 700,000. But compare the numbers using the old multiplier of 1.5, and it is a loss of nearly *3 million* members.

The AARP secretly altered its books to give themselves an overnight boost of more than two million members— without receiving a single new membership application.

Even without the "spouse factor" sleight of hand, the AARP's membership numbers are always inflated because, as one AARP official put it, it often takes "a long time for us to record that a member has died or their membership has lapsed. We've found numerous instances where our records are out of whack." Specifically responsible for calculating membership figures, she nevertheless added: "Don't believe the numbers."

ONE LEGITIMATE QUESTION: With AARP's membership so huge, does it really matter if they've dropped a few million members in recent years?

To the AARP leaders, it's a serious crisis, though they are unlikely to admit this in public. First, it indicates a trend that is accelerating with the baby boomers. And second, they know that Congress follows this closely. Admitting a three-million-membership drop in three years will mean a serious diminishment of impact for their lobbyists. "It's a *perception* of power that gets them in the door in the first place," one Congressional Democratic staffer says. "If we get the perception that their members are leaving in droves, and they're hiding that with some accounting shenanigans, believe me, it will have an effect up here."

Another reason AARP officials are so internally alarmed about the drop is the huge loss in *income* this represents. "Names spell dollars," one staffer put it pithily. Losing three million members means losing up to $24 million in membership fees and an estimated $1.35 *billion* in gross revenues for the AARP's business partners.

WHEN IT COMES TO RECRUITMENT, the AARP has to run fast just to stay in place: the more members who leave, the more new members are needed to replace them to stay even. Every month, membership expires for an average one million members, and they must be persuaded to renew or must be replaced by new members.

One possible solution, argued by Membership Development analysts in senior staff meetings, holds that if the AARP really wants more members, the association should spend yet more money on advertising and solicitation. But with 48 percent of the over-fifty population already AARP members, the law of diminishing returns inevitably kicks in. It will be increasingly expensive to obtain new customers.

Another potential solution is to lower the membership age to forty-five to increase the "membership universe," as AARP puts it. But this, apparently, has never been seriously considered. "The age of 50 was selected by the Board and determined as the age for membership. I know of no decision or movement to 45," says Anne Harvey, chief of the Programs Division. Offered spokesperson Tom Otwell: "Most 40-year-olds don't think about retirement, but 50 is certainly that magic age."

A third route is to offer new incentives to keep the customers they already have. The AARP has been quietly testing several ideas like encouraging members to pay their dues with credit cards and offering members ten or twenty minutes of free, prepaid long-distance telephone calling if they renew for three or ten years, respectively.

More to the point than these gimmicks is finding out why one-fifth of AARP's membership chooses not to renew every year. "This patient is very sick, and no one wants to call the doctor," says a Membership Division official. "Find the symptoms, prescribe the cure." In fact, the division has identified four primary reasons for members not renewing. One wag calls them, "the killer D's—*death, disinterest, dues* and *dissent.*"

The death of members is unavoidable. Only God can prevent the AARP from losing at least a million members a year to what AARP records call an "involuntary lapse." The loss is actually higher than the AARP records show, because it can take years before the AARP acknowledges that someone is dead. "We keep them on until somebody like the U.S. Postal Service notifies us or their subscription runs out," explains one AARP data processing official. Even when the AARP gets the information, it is sometimes lost or entered incorrectly. "We have no vested interest in removing a member from our numbers, particularly if we've already got his or her money," he added.

One of the more remarkable examples of this is the account of the trials and travails of Donald Helwig, Mount Vernon, Washington, who tells it best in his own words:[4]

My experience with AARP has not been a good one and has lead me to believe that it is an organization fraught with waste and bureaucratic confusion. I also believe that their reported membership numbers are highly exaggerated.

Previous to 1985 both of my parents received AARP mailings— always duplicated because each received the same mailing. Two copies of *Modern Maturity* magazine and duplicates of everything else! After mother passed away in 1985 my father asked me to help him get her mailings discontinued. It took months and much frustration.

In 1990, my father passed away. I notified AARP and sent a copy of the death certificate. It worked great... now they sent all of his mail to his name and MY ADDRESS. I contacted the magazine independently; it did not help. In addition, I now began to receive the magazine myself. Now, I was getting dad's copy and my copy. I wrote to the AARP again, but nothing changed.

In March of 1991, I moved to the state of Washington. I forwarded only my First Class mail. My magazine stopped; after about three months, my father's AARP mailings began to arrive at my Washington address. I obtained several more AARP addresses and wrote to them all, trying to get him off their lists. I finally had to write a NASTY letter to the director.

Would you believe that the mailings to my father stopped? The next month, the AARP mailed the *Modern Maturity* and some additional publications to MY MOTHER at my address.

If the AARP continues to carry all the names of all the people who have passed away, there have to be thousands of copies wasted. There have to be thousands of names on their lists of members who are deceased. Who is paying the bills?

I am now 62 years old, but there is no way I want to ever get on their mailing lists. The "junk" mailings every month are astounding. If AARP provides a service to someone, just be sure it isn't to me. I want no part of them.

MANY MEMBERS LEAVE because they don't find anything in AARP interesting or useful to them. "The organization hasn't met their expectations," former division chief Wayne Haefer puts it. "They just didn't see this organization as relevant in meeting their needs at the current time." The loss of members has been the subject of the typical expensive, confidential, annual AARP surveys—this one called the "Lapsed Members Study." A recent one[5] (1995), which asked the nonrenewers to check off one or more reasons why they dropped out, found that lack of interest ranked highest:

- I didn't use any AARP services, or AARP services didn't meet my needs. (48 percent)

- I did not receive any benefits from membership. (37 percent)

- I overlooked or neglected renewing. (26 percent)

- Discounts or savings on AARP services were not as much as I expected. (19 percent)

OBVIOUSLY, MANY MEMBERS of AARP are ambivalent about their membership. Many more are apathetic. How else can one explain this clumsy finding from AARP's 1993 Lapsed Members Study:[6] "About three-quarters of lapsed members were satisfied with their AARP membership."

A telling "lapsed member" is Walter Hoffmann of Versailles, Kentucky. Hoffmann was one of the AARP's most celebrated members. He was selected to be their twenty millionth. At fifty-eight, he had retired three years before from Rand McNally, where he had been manager of the bindery section and a production account executive. His name "emerged" in a "random" sample from among the thirty thousand who joined one week in September 1985.[7]

AARP treated him and his wife, Virginia, like royalty for a week that December. They were flown free to Washington, D.C., and put up in a wonderful hotel. They visited with top AARP leaders, toured Washington, met powerful congressmen, and were finally whisked to the Oval Office for a chat with President Ronald Reagan. All of this was faithfully photographed and reported by the AARP.

"We really had a grand time in Washington," recalls Mrs. Hoffmann a decade later in an interview with the author. "It was very exciting."

Did you get any pictures?

"Well, they did take lots and lots of pictures, but we never received any—at least from AARP. We did get some from the White House, but not AARP. They took lots of pictures and they said they were going to send us a video, too, but we never heard from them."

Did they ever contact you again?

"Well, they did send a short response after we sent a letter of thanks for our nice visit in Washington," she laughed.

Are you still members of the AARP?

"No," she laughed again. "We just didn't renew our subscription this past year."

Any reason?

"Well, we had originally joined AARP because it offered travel discounts. But now they don't offer that anymore. We had applied once for some kind of insurance but we were turned down or the price was too high. Anyway, there wasn't too much in there that we were interested in...."

BUT THE AARP'S GREATEST FEAR isn't losing old members, it is becoming irrelevant to new ones. As former AARP public affairs chief Martha Welsh puts it: "Can we go from FDR to Woodstock?"[8]

So far, the answer has been a resounding *no*. "When I first came to work here [in the late 1980s], they were always saying, 'How are we ever going to accommodate all those boomers? There are so many of them. We're going to have to double the size of the organization to serve them!' But all that talk has gone away," observed a staffer in the personnel department. "It's not going the way they [upper management] had thought it would go with the boomers," agrees long-time AARP staffer Lee Pearson.[9] "Unfortunately we have a lot of non-interested young boomers."

And it is no wonder. As one former staffer told me, "There is a natural tension between the older members and the younger members, but every time, the leadership always err on the side of the over 65." The evidence of this is everywhere. Publications are filled with articles on Social Security and Medicare, for which the under 65 are not eligible. The premiere product—AARP group health insurance sold by Prudential—is a Medigap policy; they have no group health insurance for those under 65. Virtually the only issues specifically useful to the fifty to sixty-five age group are a small number of workforce initiatives the AARP has. But these have neither been prominent, nor caught on with AARP's younger members. So the AARP staff and the Board continue to concentrate on making the older members happy. And that's going to cost them members aplenty. The first baby boomers to hit sixty-five won't do so until 2011.

In fact, the normal differences between those over sixty-five and those under sixty-five appear even more pronounced with the coming baby boomer segment—almost a breed apart, according to Melinda Halpert.[10] "They [boomers] are not a generation of readers, so we'll be experimenting with all kinds of alternative media to reach them. It's almost like an anthropologist discovering a new breed of mankind. They're a positive influence, a generation that's dependent on quality. But they're also more cynical, which makes it tougher to communicate with them." Metaphorically, the boomers are plugged into their "Walkmen" and would rather listen to the racous sounds of fellow boomer Mick Jagger than to the come-ons of Horace Deets.

The third of the "Ds" killing off AARP membership—after death and disinterest—are the dues it charges. Though some would regard AARP's dues as nominal at less than $10, every time the Association raises them, it loses members.

AARP's dues started at $2 a year, gradually rising to $5 in 1982. In September 1992, with some apologia, AARP's dues rose to $8 a year. Executive Director Horace Deets explained to the members that "our operating costs have been rising along with everybody else's."[11] (True enough, but a *big* factor was the need for cash to pay the AARP's impending $135 million settlement with the IRS.)

Many older Americans feel they cannot afford the $8 a year membership fee. In one survey,[12] the AARP found that 12 percent of older Americans polled "cite expense as the reason for not joining." According to the same survey, one-quarter of those who choose not to renew their membership cite as the cause: "I could not afford to renew my membership."

When so many members are ambivalent about AARP membership anyway, it only takes a small issue like this to push them off the fence. "To be honest, I never thought they did too much for me. I often said if they ever raised the subscription of $5, I would cancel my subscription," R.A. Vierling of Yreka, California, wrote.[13] "When they went to $8, I did exactly that."

Another chunk of AARP's fence-sitting members leave the organization simply to avoid the deluge of junk mail AARP sends out. In the 1995 lapsed members study, 12 percent gave as a reason for dropping their membership: "There were too many mailings."

Former AARP member and activist Ted Ruhig chuckles about this. "Some people say 'Gee whiz, when we pay our annual membership dues to AARP, we're really just putting our name on the junk mail list.' It's the only place they know of where they pay to be on the junk mailing list!"

Irma K. Smith of Sheridan, Michigan, agrees[14]: "For a few years I was a member after my fiftieth birthday. From the very beginning I was inundated with mail. Opportunities poured in. Offers for insurance coverage. For me, for my car, for my mobile home. And if the first offer wasn't enough, they followed each one up with second and third chances to reciprocate. Each time I received something from them, I thought it might be something very important about my membership, so I had to read it carefully. Always it was just a sales pitch."

THE FINAL "KILLER D" underlying the AARP's huge loss of members is a big one: Dissent. The AARP doesn't know *exactly* how many members oppose their lobbying, but they know roughly—and it's big. By far, the largest and most significant drop in the AARP's membership in the past decade occurred after the AARP supported the Medicare Catastrophic Coverage Act (1988–89) and the Mitchell–Gephardt health care reform bills (1994).

"It's a cold calculation," explains a Membership Division expert. "We tell the board time and time again, take a position on the Hill and you lose members. The more controversial, the greater the loss. The *majority* of our membership don't really have a good reason for staying with AARP, and any little excuse causes them to truck on down the road. Liberal lobbying positions are a big excuse to leave. In fact, I've never understood why we have *any* Republicans who are members of AARP, unless they find the discounts so enticing that they'll ignore our Democratic nature."

Certainly the largest group of dissenters who leave are those who are convinced that AARP's leaders are big-government and high-tax-supporting liberals who are unwilling to change. "It is important for you to understand that I am not alone in my strong feelings for my disgust at the arrogant attitude of the AARP leadership as are several of my friends who are also members," says D. Miller of Palm Bay, Florida.[15] "I am afraid that AARP has been taken over by a small cadre of radical left-thinking individuals whose arrogance and lack of respect for other viewpoints is appalling."

Some dissenters hang in as AARP members in the hope that the AARP will eventually treat its members as if they were stockholders in a corporation, and treat their complaints with appropriate concern. An angry former senior manager of AARP asserts: "I feel you can't write them nasty letters until you join. If you want to have a voice, you have to get involved."

But with the baby boomers, the problem of dissent will be even more pronounced. "I want a say rather than have someone speak for me," complained one in a closed-door AARP focus group. "Your views are not in sync with your own members," said a second. A third: "AARP is inflexible, cumbersome, like a ship in a harbor." Concluded the confidential "Stratogram" reporting on AARP's "Advocacy Image With Boomers":[16]

> By and large, there was consensus that the boomers would not now, or in the future, support the legislative record AARP prides itself on. They would support advocacy for such issues as education—a relevant need, and they would even support political action groups that met their needs and interests of the moment. Most compared AARP with AAA (American Automobile Association). In every session, just about every participant belonged to AAA, and they were quick to point out that AAA has no legislative agenda, even relating to transportation.

A later "Stratogram," sumarizing dozens of surveys and focus groups warned that:

> Often enough, respondents viewed AARP as "politically partisan"; consistently "backing liberal policy"; and having a single opinion on complex, divisive issues. These perceptions can polarize members and threaten future success only if the AARP allows itself to be put in the position of stressing conformity to any particular philosophy or position. (As an example, many Americans joined the National

Rifle Association [NRA] because they thought gun safety and education were a good idea and enjoyed their discounts. Today, the NRA's gun safety and education efforts go largely unnoticed. The NRA has created an environment where it is difficult to remain a member if your views on gun ownership and 2nd Amendment rights do not conform with the organization's.)

Factor in the boomers' and post boomers' general mistrust of traditional institutions, and you have an environment where any effort to represent a diverse membership or take a leading viewpoint on issues will be seen as a push toward conformity. Conformity to an institutional viewpoint is something these groups currently won't tolerate.

VOLUNTEER LEADER David Rogowsky uttered a like prediction at the AARP's annual meeting of top staff and volunteers in 1995:

> We have to change as an organization. We have to meet the needs of younger members who should be joining and sticking around instead of not renewing. If we don't change, and soon, AARP will become like the now defunct Eastern or Pan Am airlines—just a name everybody remembers… but doesn't exist anymore.

Without knowing it, he may have written the AARP's epitaph. In a decade or two, America's second largest organization might just fade away, its "Taj Mahal" an archtectural folly occupied by other tenants, and Deets's empire simply will not "exist anymore."

APPENDIX A

AARP's Product Lines

No organization has done a more thorough and objective review of AARP products and services than the editors and staff of the nation's largest financial publication, *Money*. Their last go-round was July 1995, when they reported the conclusions of an exhaustive project that involved nearly two dozen independent experts.[1] The products were rated on a scale of one to five, with five being the best. Altogether, the AARP scored $32^{1/2}$ out of a possible 55. "Overall, AARP's deals are slightly better than average," they concluded.

What follows now is the author's own look at the AARP, drawing from *Money*'s landmark work, dozens of interviews with AARP and "service provider" officials, outside experts, and access to AARP internal documents. Anecdotes are included from admirers and detractors.

The statistics that introduce each product are from 1994, the most recent year for which full information exists. Since I devoted two chapters to the AARP pharmacy service, I've skipped it here.

Program: **Group Health Insurance**
Partner: **Prudential Insurance Company of America (until the end of 1997, then United Healthcare, Metropolitan Life, and ITT Hartford).**
Members Participating: **5.8 million individuals**
Gross Revenue: **$3.466 billion**
AARP Cut: **$119.4 million**[2]
Grade: **B–**

AFTER MEMBERSHIP DUES, the Group Health Insurance Program is the AARP's largest single source of revenue. Prudential has underwritten and managed the program since 1981. But its contract expires at the end of 1997, and, in a stunning announcement, the AARP decided to discontinue the relationship. It's a multibillion-dollar loss for Prudential, whose special AARP program, headquartered in Fort Washington, Pennsylvania, currently employs more than 4,500 full and part-time staff. Prudential's loss is the gain of United HealthCare, Metropolitan Life, and ITT Hartford, who will take over the program.

At best, the AARP's program is a mixed blessing for the members.

The AARP's **Medicare Supplement Plans** are generally regarded as some of the best and most inexpensive ones around. Depending on the plan, they can cover Medicare-eligible expenses not paid in full by Medicare, such as prescription drugs, preventive care, and at-home health care. Few seniors can go wrong with these policies.

Generally, they are least advantageous for older men, and the most beneficial for older women. The AARP "community rates" its plans, which means the premiums don't go up as the insured person gets older. So the AARP's Medigap plans are a real steal if you're older than seventy. But younger men are paying more than they would in comparable non–AARP policies.

The reviews for the AARP's other insurance policies aren't nearly as positive.

The AARP's main **Hospital Indemnity Plan**, for example, is universally lampooned as a total waste of money. "No matter how old you are, stay away," urged *Money* magazine.

The truth is that hospital supplement policies are always a bad bargain, despite elderly consumer demand for them. Many experts fault the AARP for even offering them, and suggest they should take the high road and explain why they don't make sense.

The general hospital plan pays small benefits for relatively lower premiums. When members are actually hospitalized, they are routinely disappointed at how little is reimbursed. AARP member Zolton M. Varga of Warren, Maine, related how he was hospitalized in 1993 for a prostate operation.[3] "The total bill came to about $8,000. Of this, Medicare paid $7,000, I paid close to $600 and AARP paid about $400+. At the time, I had faithfully paid monthly premiums to the AARP plan for eight years."

The more limited hospital indemnity plan for members between the ages of fifty and sixty-four makes more sense if you are not already covered by an employer's plan, which is bound to be better. The AARP's "Hospital Advantage Plans" provide partial benefit payments for hospitalization, doctor visits, home health care, and surgical procedures. Coverage is based on past history. Smokers, for example, will pay a higher premium than nonsmokers.

Also near the bottom of the heap is the AARP's **Long-Term Care Insurance**. Available to members from ages fifty to seventy-nine, this pricey policy pays daily benefits for home health care, adult day care, and extended nursing home stays. But unless you're very poor *and* can't qualify for Medicaid, other insurers provide far more comprehensive long-term coverage for much lower premiums.[4]

Program: **Auto/Homeowners' Insurance**
Partner: **ITT Hartford**
Members Participating: **1.6 million policyholders**
Gross Revenue: **$1,042 billion**
AARP Cut: **$25 million**
Grade: **C+**

AS WITH THE AARP'S lucrative group health insurance program, it is not clear in its auto and home insurance which comes first—business interests or the members' interests.

For example, J. Robert Hunter, president of the National Insurance Consumer Organization, was once invited to advise AARP staffers on how they could get lower premium rates for their members. Hunter learned later that some of the attendees worked for Hartford, the company charging the high premiums that AARP supposedly wanted to lower. After Hunter complained, AARP officials said Hunter misunderstood the purpose of the meeting. It was an "information" session, not a "strategy" session.[5]

The AARP's auto and home insurance gets mixed reviews. A subscriber can save money by signing up for both services, but the **auto insurance** policy in particular gets poor marks.

The AARP auto plan is meant to be inexpensive, but only for those who don't drive much. And Hartford is slow to forgive its policyholders for accidents or traffic violations.

The strength of the AARP auto policy is that policyholders are guaranteed that their insurance will not be canceled just because they get old—a universal fear of the elderly that was one of the motivating forces behind the founding of the service in 1984. An AARP member can be dropped only by Hartford for drunk driving, failure to pay premiums, or if a doctor determines that the senior is no longer fit to drive.

But the guarantee of continued coverage is not a guarantee of continued discounts. Auto premium rates go up as the policyholder ages, a fact that grates on some who think the AARP should be the one place where someone is not penalized for getting older.

Moreover, a guarantee of renewal doesn't mean that AARP/Hartford will agree to cover an applicant in the first place. Ernest Ryder, an AARP member from Raymond, Maine, was refused coverage by Hartford because he drove thirty thousand miles a year.[6] Apparently he didn't fit the profile of the little old man who took the car out of the garage only once a week to go to church. Similarly, George and Doris Dolaptchieff of Ocean Park, Washington, ages sixty-five and sixty-two, respectively, were denied coverage by Hartford because they owned a vehicle that was a bit too youthful—a four-wheel-drive Jeep Wrangler.[7] Gladys Mann of Ogden, Utah, was denied Hartford coverage because she had a cataract in one eye. She sent two statements from doctors saying that her vision was corrected to 20/20 with glasses, but Hartford still wouldn't insure her.[8]

The AARP/Hartford **homeowners' insurance**, on the other hand, can be a better deal than Allstate's or State Farm's, though it depends on where the insured member resides.

James Maas of Berkeley, California, for example, called for a price quote, which turned out to be as much as 50 percent higher than he was already paying for insurance. Maas complained in a letter to AARP, and he thinks others must have complained, too, because the AARP's ads changed from "Now You Can Save Money with the New AARP Homeowners' Insurance Program…" to "Can the new AARP Homeowners' Insurance Program give you better protection—at a better price?"[9] Sometimes the answer is *no*.

Program: **Mobile Home Insurance**
Partner: **Foremost Insurance Group**
Members Participating: **113,000 policyholders**
Gross Revenue: **$34 million**
AARP Cut: **$1.7 million**
Grade: **A–**

THOUGH IT HAS BEEN in operation since 1990, this is the AARP's least-known member service program.

Nevertheless, it is an excellent buy in most states. In fact, in the first four years it was *too good* a buy. Unlike other insurers, AARP/Foremost automatically included earthquake, flood, and hurricane coverage in areas where others charged additionally for it. But the insurers took it on the chin for this, according to a series of confidential AARP reports. For instance, they suffered $4 million in losses from the 1994 Los Angeles earthquake. Interestingly, according to one report, many of those losses "occurred in one park, where half of the units were insured by Foremost and were high-value homes. Foremost has had a team of loss adjusters on site since the day following the quake."[10]

Foremost was forced to start ratcheting up the premiums a bit, and including higher payments in those areas that suffer routinely from natural disasters. But it is still pretty much the best buy in most states—and this, even though acts of God continue to decimate the profit line. Winter storms and flooding in the first quarter of 1996 caused the second highest quarter losses for the plan, with the highest still being the third quarter of 1994 when Hurricane Andrew ripped through Florida and tossed mobile homes around like matchsticks.[11]

Program: **Motoring Plan**
Partner: **Amoco**
Members Participating: **900,000 households**
Gross Revenue: **$38 million**
AARP Cut: **$1.9 million**
Grade: **B+**

SINCE 1980 THE AARP has offered an auto club plan to its members using the Amoco Motor Club. The annual dues are $39.95, and the package is generally comparable to other auto clubs, offering towing, roadside assistance, and trip planning services. The AARP/Amoco service is generally good, but cannot match that of the American Automobile Association (AAA), which has about twice as many participating service stations.

In December 1995 the Signature Group bought the Amoco Motor Club and is expected to make some changes. In a confidential summary of a Spring 1996 survey, it concluded that the "AARP Motoring Plan performance in the area of road service is comparable to that of AAA, with 86 percent of AARP Motoring Plan participants and 92 percent of AAA participants reporting being satisfied."[14] But the map/trip routing service was still substandard, with only 79 percent being satisfied with the AARP's service compared to 95 percent with AAA's service.

Program: **Purchase Privilege Program**
Partners: **Avis, Hertz, National**
Members Participating: **1.7 million**
Gross Revenue: **$90 million**
AARP Cut: **$4.5 million**
Grade: **B+**

LODGING AND CAR rental discounts are the best known of all the AARP "member services."[13]

Officially called the "Purchase Privilege Program," the discounts began in 1972 with the Sheraton, Marriott, and Rodeway hotel chains. Now more than two dozen chains are part of the program. The AARP calculates that 32 percent of its members use the lodging discount a year. More important to the AARP is the car rental portion of the Purchase Privilege Program. The AARP receives no royalties from the hotel discount program, but it does receive 5 percent of the price paid by AARP members to rent Avis, Hertz, or National vehicles. Unfortunately for the AARP, only 5 percent of its members know about and use this program—or about one-sixth the number who use the lodging discounts. Still, it represents an increasingly useful source of revenue for the association.[14]

The AARP's travel and car rental discounts are good values because they come automatically with the annual $8 membership fee. In particular, fifty- to sixty-year-old members benefit, because they would not normally qualify for "senior" discounts.

Some AARP members complain that the better AARP discounts are quite restrictive. "It sounds good in small print, or even in large print, but does not hold true in actuality," reported Awbrey Norris of Winter Springs, Florida.[15] "Example: Large metropolitan hotel, national chain, AARP discounts. 1000 rooms or more. No AARP discount available. Why? BOTH ROOMS with AARP discounts were taken for the night. Figure that out! I did get a better room, 20 percent less in rate, by being a Delta Airlines Frequent Flyer. Age had nothing to do with it."

The AARP frequently advertises that its lodging discounts go as high as 50 percent. But their rooms are extremely limited, they must be booked at least twenty-one days in advance, and pre-payment is required at the time of reservation.

Another complaint is that the AARP discount is the same for any "senior" over fifty-five or sixty. "Seniors do not need to belong to AARP to get the benefit," declares Marvin O. Webber of Middletown, Indiana.[16] "The senior discount is offered to seniors regardless of AARP membership," agreed G.M. Durham of Montrose, Colorado.[17]

Some seniors have moral qualms about the discounts. "We get small discounts when we travel, but we have felt bad about it," says Janice Miskie of Reading, Pennsylvania. "Why should we get discounts when our children are struggling so and are not entitled to any discounts anywhere!"[18]

One former AARP member from Roswell, New Mexico, adds, "What about the young families, the young children? Is everything to be sacrificed so senior citizens can get in their RVs and tour the country, traveling on Social Security, finding discounts in everything from where they eat to where they camp in National Parks? To me, AARP stands for the mindless hordes who are forever running around our country, taking vacations two, three, or four times a year, living it up on the backs of the young. AARP is getting all this for them. I think we need a new organization for the young called ATPFI—Association for Those Paying For It!"

Program: **Visa/Mastercard**
Partner: **Bank One**
Members Participating: **1.2 million cardholders**
Gross Revenue: **at least $65.25 million**[19]
AARP Cut: **$8.7 million**
Grade: **D**

WHEN THE AARP'S Federal Credit Union folded in 1990, the only operation worth picking out of the rubble was the Visa credit card program administered by Bank One of Ohio, which was then expanded to include MasterCard.

As of mid-1996, the majority of AARP credit cardholders (1,147,764) preferred the Visa Classic card with a $10 annual fee, $5,000 credit line, and 15.15 percent interest rate. Another 164,928 opted for the no-fee MasterCard Classic, with its $5,000 credit line and 17.9 percent interest rate. Finally, 89,942 were signed up for the Visa Gold card that charged the same interest rate as the Visa Classic, but asked a $15 annual fee for a $7,500 credit line.[20] AARP cardholders are expected soon to have the option of carrying a "PhotoCard."[21] Increasingly, the AARP's cut in all this is based on charges the members make. The more debt they accrue, the more money the AARP pulls in.

While the ads in AARP publications have a "come one, come all" lure about them, these cards are not so easy to come by. The turn-down rate for applicants is high—by some estimates 40 percent to

50 percent. The AARP touts the cards as an opportunity for the elderly, especially women, to jump on the credit bandwagon. AARP officials like to point out that instead of just relying on a check of credit history, which many from the pay-as-you-go generation don't have, the AARP cards will qualify an applicant based on net worth.

Yet anecdotes abound of AARP members who applied for Bank One credit cards and were turned down for the same reasons that other banks turn down applicants—slim or no credit history, lack of home ownership, or a recent move.

Jim Clayton, an AARP member from Knoxville, Tennessee, was rejected because he had just moved to a new house. Nobody offered him the option of filling out a net-worth statement. But Clayton finally got his credit card when he sent Bank One a copy of his 1991 tax return. It turns out that this particular AARP member was one of the richest people in America, number 399 on the Forbes 400 list, a mobile home magnate with a net worth of $265 million. Clayton had indeed made a recent move—a red flag for credit card issuers. But he had gone from one house to another in a development that he built. That was good enough for Bank One, which sent him his Visa card, an apology, and "enough flowers to bury me with."[22]

An AARP employee who made a private hobby of tracking Bank One denials found the company was not so kind to AARP members who were not multimillionaires. A woman who owned two homes in upper class communities was turned down for lack of a credit history. The credit cards had always been in her husband's name, and now he was dead and she was considered a poor risk. Another woman called from her room in a nursing home, crying because the AARP had denied her a credit card. Others sent angry letters, complaining that they had joined the AARP only to get the credit card, and were insulted at being turned down.[23]

To offset some of this resentment, the AARP and Bank One are currently experimenting with a Secured Card that requires AARP members with poor credit histories to put up a deposit equal to the credit line on the credit card account.[24]

Program: **Mutual Funds**
Partner: **Scudder, Stevens & Clark, Incorporated**
Members Participating: **800,000 accounts**
AARP Assets Under Management: **$11.1 billion**
Gross Revenue: **$83 million**
AARP Cut: **$7.6 million**
Grade: **B–**

FOR AARP, the theory behind selling mutual funds is rather straight-forward: keep it safe and simple.

While many mutual fund programs are difficult to understand and require investors to have the nerves of a high-stakes gambler, the AARP carefully explains its offerings to potential investors and assures them that their money will be invested in relatively low risk stocks and bonds. This philosophy surely endears seniors to the "AARP Investment Program" that has been operated for the AARP since 1985 by Scudder, Stevens & Clark, Incorporated.[25] But as those who are familiar with the art of investing know well, low risk often means low returns. Such is the case with many of the AARP's funds.

That doesn't mean that the AARP doesn't benefit, though. Members currently entrust the AARP-Scudder investment program with more than $12 billion of their private savings.[26] AARP's yearly "take" from this investing has steadily climbed from $1.6 million to $7.6 million between 1989 and 1994. The AARP cut is funneled to AARP through a taxable, for-profit organization jointly run by the AARP and Scudder, called the AARP Financial Services Corporation.

Scudder is able to promote the mutual funds exclusively to AARP members through the association's various publications, such as *Modern Maturity*. The AARP does not allow other mutual funds programs to advertise in its publications, giving Scudder a distinct advantage with seniors.

The AARP offers seniors a family of eight mutual funds to choose from. None will produce huge returns for investors, and a few aren't worth the price of admission. Here's a brief look (using 1994 asset figures):

The AARP GNMA and U.S. Treasury and **AARP Growth & Income** are generally considered the two best AARP funds. Not incidentally, they are number one and two in investor interest. AARP members have parked $5.243 billion in the GNMA/Treasury fund, and $2.3 billion in Growth & Income. Both have delivered steady returns to investors over the past several years, and neither is very risky. AARP Growth & Income is particularly good for those looking for a solid, long-term investment.

The third favorite, the **AARP Insured Tax-Free General Bond**, has not performed as well as comparable municipal bond funds, but Scudder has now changed its investment strategy, so it might improve. It holds $1.745 billion in member assets.

The AARP Capital Growth Fund is the most aggressive of AARP's mutual fund offerings. But many seniors prefer to play it safe. Experts are telling would-be investors to stay away—over the past few years returns have been negligible. Still, members have installed $630 million in assets here.

The **AARP's High-Quality Bond Fund** doesn't live up to its name. In recent years, it's been much more unpredictable than comparable funds offered by others, but $528 million is invested in this group.

The AARP High-Quality Money Fund and the **AARP High-Quality Tax-Free Money Fund** are also of questionable value. Neither compares well with similar funds offered by others, but hold $378 million and $131.5 million in member assests, respectively.

The **AARP Balanced Stock and Bond Fund** is the newest AARP offering, holding $178 million in member assets. It has received rave reviews so far, returning more to investors than the average fund of its kind.

With so many mutual funds out there—including other Scudder ones that outperform the AARP group—the association has anything but a corner on the market. Even the most prosperous funds aren't that much better than their competitors. Seniors looking to invest should be wary of the AARP's spin doctors.

Other Services

THE AARP HAS MADE a recent foray into the life insurance business, signing up New York Life Insurance Company to cater policies to AARP members. More than sixty-five thousand members have signed on to the program in its first year, in spite of significant drawbacks to the policy. Death benefits are low, ranging only from $13,800 to $25,000. And the price is high for women and healthy men who normally get breaks from other insurance companies.

There are advantages to the AARP plan: No physical exam is required, and subscribers cannot be dropped once they join. If the insured person lands in a nursing home for more than 180 days, New York Life will waive future premiums. But these pluses aren't enough to offset the negatives. There are better buys from other vendors for AARP members.

Also in 1995 the AARP launched an annuity program to favorable reviews in the financial press. To run the program, the AARP formed a joint venture called "American Maturity Life Insurance Company" in partnership with ITT Hartford and Pacific Mutual.

An annuity is like a life insurance policy, but it pays the holder as long as he or she doesn't die. The investor pays premiums, and then the interest is tax-deferred until the retiree begins to withdraw money from the account. The AARP version of annuities has some advantages over the norm. The minimum premium to sign on is $5,000—lower than many annuity plans—and the salespeople work on a salary instead of a commission, which means the elderly don't have to worry about being bulldozed by an aggressive sales pitch.

In the first eighteen months of the program, the AARP sold more than 1,300 policies, representing more than $36.5 million in premiums invested by AARP members, according to internal documents.

The AARP is also currently experimenting with low-cost dental and vision insurance, and discounted legal services.

"AARP makes available a new program only after we determine that the program will be of special value to its members and that the program is consistent with AARP's goal to serve older Americans," insists Communications Division Director James Holland.[27]

Yeah, and he's got a bridge over in Brooklyn to sell the members because they have a special need to cross the water, too. In her internal paper on an AARP model "to develop new offerings/new products," AARP senior staffer Kathy Hardy wrote that the "Business Analysis" was most pivotal. "Estimate possible revenue and costs by different levels of demand."[28] As another document testifies: "The mission of Membership Services Operations is to provide AARP members with programs that respond to their needs and provide value and distinctiveness not otherwise generally available, backed by the highest level of service, and in doing so, earn revenue for AARP."

So there it is: if AARP can't make money on a product, it doesn't matter how badly some members want or need it. As was seen in the cases of the AARP travel program and federal credit union, AARP will shut down a money-losing program faster than you can say "failure".

APPENDIX B

AARP's Competitors

The NATIONAL COUNCIL on AGING (NCOA), a frequent friend of the AARP, is the granddaddy of the senior organizations. Founded in 1950, it now boasts seven thousand members. The NCOA keeps a low profile and lobbies for select causes, including housing, employment, adult day care, and health care.[1]

More high-brow than some of its low-rent competitors, NCOA sponsors conferences that are decidedly academic in tone and publishes journals to keep its members up to date on the latest ruminations in the field of gerontology. NCOA also runs a travel agency and mail-order pharmacy for its members, and offers group health insurance and discounts on hotels and rental cars. The NCOA gets more than $35 million in federal grant money every year to run senior employment programs.[2]

The **NATIONAL COUNCIL of SENIOR CITIZENS** is an occasional friend of AARP, depending on how liberal AARP's stand is on a particular issue. The NCSC is not coy about its own politics. It is decidedly left of center.

The organization was born in 1961 in the offices of the AFL-CIO. Its purpose then was to lobby for the creation of Medicare in the face of heavily funded opposition from the American Medical Association and the AARP itself. In a big sendoff, the NCSC's first convention drew twenty thousand people and featured as its guest speaker President John F. Kennedy. The organization can rightly take credit for being the strongest nongovernment advocate of Medicare in that early fight.[3]

Today, it remains loyal to its organized labor roots and counts five million members—all seniors who belong to various unions under the umbrella of the AFL-CIO. NCSC presidents are always top union bosses.

It claims five million members, but only five hundred thousand actually open their wallets to pay dues. Still, the NCSC can legitimately call itself the third largest senior lobby in Congress after the AARP and the National Committee to Preserve Social Security and Medicare.

More than 90 percent of the NCSC operating budget comes from federal grants.

Occasionally, a conservative member of Congress, fired up by senior groups that resent the grant money going to AARP and NCSC, will attempt legislation to ban tax-exempt lobby groups from getting federal grants. But so far those attempts have failed.

Unfettered as yet by any such regulation, NCSC has stood up against Medicare reform, especially if it means any cut in spending. The organization actively opposed the North American Free Trade Agreement, and GOP budget cutting measures. During the 1994 health care reform debate, NCSC took the position that Hillary

Clinton's package was a good beginning, but not nearly close enough to total nationalized health care. NCSC favored something more like the Canadian single-payer system. NCSC's former executive director Lawrence Smedley said the 104th Congress's "Contract with America" was an "economic suicide pact."

The AARP and NCSC are frequent allies, but in the fight over catastrophic health insurance coverage for seniors in 1989, NCSC parted ways with the AARP, and some hard feelings remain. NCSC's primary mission is political, and its members know that. "Our membership is much more politically active," Burns has said. "We're unabashedly to the left...."[4]

Because it has a secure income stream from the federal government, NCSC's top leadership rebukes other senior organizations that are constantly dunning their members. Smedley called his competitors "liars for hire," when they used scare tactics to spook their members into giving more money.[5]

The **NATIONAL COMMITTEE TO PRESERVE SOCIAL SECURITY and MEDICARE** was founded in 1982 by Butcher Forde Consulting Company, a California direct mail outfit.

In its first year, it sucked in $1.7 million from its members. Within a few years of its inception, the National Committee was raking in $30 million a year from mailings that frequently gave vulnerable seniors the impression that their Social Security checks were in jeopardy. In a 1987 congressional hearing on direct mail excesses, Social Security Commissioner Dorcas Hardy called the National Committee "irresponsible" for scaring the elderly. Thirty-one members of the House signed a letter criticizing the National Committee for its methods.

In 1989 the National Committee led the fight to repeal the catastrophic health care bill, with a catchy shorthand name for the law—the "seniors-only tax."

The National Committee moved on to exploit the "notch babies"—people born between 1917 and 1926 who receive lower Social Security benefits than those born before them. When the formula for

computing benefits was changed in 1977 there was an error, and people born between 1910 and 1917 are getting $132 a month more. The
AARP neglected the notch issue, thus angering some members who
joined National Committee, which pushed for higher benefits for all.

For years, the National Committee was not invited to speak at
Capitol Hill. But the group finally won the affections of Florida
Congressman Claude Pepper and Arizona Senator John McCain. The
cachet of those two names, both elected from senior strongholds,
gave the National Committee a toehold on the Hill, and that hold has
strengthened, with its contribution to congressional campaigns.

The **SENIORS COALITION, UNITED SENIORS ASSOCIATION,**
and **60/PLUS** were all spun from Richard Viguerie, the right-wing
direct mail entrepreneur, though he is no longer tied to the Seniors
Coalition, and United Seniors is run by a Viguerie protége, Sandra
Butler. 60/Plus offers as a membership perk a bumper-sticker that
reads: "AARP: Association *Against* Retired Persons." It claims a
membership of 225,000. United Seniors claims 400,000 members.

The Seniors Coalition now claims a membership of more than one
million, but less than half of them pay the group's dues. The remain-
der are "supporters" who have at some point responded to a Seniors
Coalition appeal by mail or have signed a petition for the group.

Even after severing ties with Viguerie, the Seniors Coalition still
continued to put a huge amount of what it raised back into its own
administrative operations. In 1993, for example, the group's tax fil-
ings showed that it raised $11 million, and put 80 percent of it back
into more fund-raising.

The Seniors Coalition staffers frequently find themselves admitting the mistakes of the past while asserting that the group has
turned over a new leaf. Indeed, respectability came with the partial
break from Viguerie's influence. The weekly Capitol Hill newspaper
Roll Call named the coalition as one of the ten most influential lobbying groups on the Hill, but the coalition was initially slow to get
into the lobbying business. During the battle to repeal the catastrophic coverage act, the Seniors Coalition boasted to its members

that it had a full-time lobbyist working on the issue on Capitol Hill. Yet, at the time, the group had no registered lobbyist. When asked who the alleged lobbyist might be, then-executive director Jake Hansen replied sheepishly, "I guess that would be me." He said he was "in the process" of registering and "may have to eat a little crow."[6] He registered as a lobbyist a month later, but it was another two years before the full organization was registered as a lobby.

Still, the group fights for notice from members of Congress. In 1994 Paul Bramell, who was then CEO of the Seniors Coalition, complained that the group was playing second fiddle to the AARP in the debate over a balanced budget amendment to the Constitution. Bramell chaffed because Senator Paul Simon consulted the Seniors Coalition on the issue by calling the coalition office on a car phone while he was on the way over to the AARP building for a face-to-face chat.[7]

Neither the Seniors Coalition nor the AARP even pretends to be cordial with the other. From time to time, they take public swipes at each other in the press and in their own publications, or exchange testy letters whining about how one has maligned the other.

These are only a handful of the three dozen or more senior advocacy groups working in Washington. Who's hot and who's not depends largely on the political makeup of Congress. Still it's hard not to agree with Edgar D. Mock, Jr., an AARP member from Doylestown, Pennsylvania, who says that "Like everything else, the AARP needs competition from another senior group." That group will have to be big, and let us hope it will also be more altruistic than the AARP—uninterested in keeping a hand in the federal cookie jar and uninterested in filching a few bucks from seniors' pockets.

NOTES

CHAPTER 1
1. "AARP at center of struggle for power, money," David Dahl, *St. Petersburg Times*, October 9, 1994, 1.

CHAPTER 2
1. Letter to author, April 5, 1994.
2. "AARP has a duty to protect workers," Horace Deets in "As We See It" columns *AARP Bulletin*, October 1991, 3.
3. Letter to author, May 12, 1994.
4. Associated Press, as reported in the Dubuque, Iowa, *Telegraph Herald*, May 29, 1996.
5. "Suit Preaches That AARP Practiced Age Discrimination," Jan Crawford Greenburg, *Chicago Tribune*, June 6, 1996, 1.

CHAPTER 3
1. Letter to author, April 5, 1994.
2. Author interview, June 11, 1994.
3. Author interview, September 21, 1995.

CHAPTER 4
1. As quoted in "The Power Elite," *Regardies*, January 1989.
2. Author interview, April 2, 1995.
3. "Washington's Second Most Powerful Man," Jeffrey H. Birnbaum, *Fortune*, May 12, 1997, 122.

4. *Boston Globe*, February 26, 1989.

5. *Investor's Business Daily*, August 12, 1993.

6. *Regardie's*, January 1991.

7. Author interview of Katharine "Kitty" Deets, August 22, 1996.

8. Author interview of John Deets, September 4, 1996.

9. From the 1956 student annual, *Miscellany*, as related by Johnny Lou Emory, Bishop England High School librarian, August 22, 1996.

10. Author interview of John Lavelle, Charleston, South Carolina, September 4, 1996.

11. Author interview of Horace Deets, April 1, 1994.

12. AARP submission to the Internal Revenue Service, Form 990, August 15, 1996.

13. AARP press release, January 27, 1988.

14. As quoted in *The Clergy: Gatekeepers for the Future, A Guidebook*, AARP, March 1993.

15. Interview with author, August 27, 1996.

16. Horace Deets memo to Robert Covais, April 4, 1995.

17. Letter to Horace Deets from The Rev. James K. Healy, Pastor, Queen of Peace Church, Arlington, Virginia, December 14, 1994.

18. Four-page memo from the AARP Grievance Board in the Covais case, June 26, 1996.

19. Author interview, April 1, 1994.

20. Internal May 1, 1995, memo, Office of the Executive Director, including minutes for April 18, 1995, Senior Staff Meeting.

21. The new space on the second floor of Building B consisted of several rooms. Training Room A seats ninety at round tables and can be subdivided into three separate training areas. Training Room B seats seventy-eight at round tables and can be subdivided into two separate areas. All tables are folding, allowing the room to be set up in other configurations. These rooms are angular in shape to minimize the distance from the speaker to the back of the room; their walls are covered in a densely woven grey fabric that will allow either tape or pins to be used to hang materials. In addition, the Feedback/Preview

Room seats twelve to sixteen persons. Service areas include restrooms, two telephone rooms, a copier area, a serving lounge for buffet services, coat storage area for approximately 180 persons, and a reception/break area with seating for twenty to twenty-five persons.

CHAPTER 5

1. Letter to author, March 26, 1994.
2. Letter to author, April 2, 1994.
3. AARP oral history interview of Martha Morgan, former AARP Area Director, April 30, 1990.
4. AARP oral history interview of William Fitch, July 11, 1988.
5. AARP oral history interview of Ernest Giddings, July 12, 1988.
6. Unpublished manuscript, AARP archives, written in 1962.
7. *Power of Years*, 88.
8. *Story of AARP*, 11. Margaret Abrams, AARP-produced history, 1971.
9. *Power of Years*, 90.
10. AARP oral history interview of Ruth Lana, February 1, 1988, as part of an internal AARP history project.
11. *Power of Years*, 36.
12. Ibid, 209–210.
13. Ibid, 217.
14. Ibid, 303–306.
15. Executive Director's Report, *AARP Bulletin*, March 1988.
16. Horace Deets interview with author, April 1, 1994.
17. Lehrmann convention address, May 4, 1994.

CHAPTER 6

1. Author interview of Sen. Alan K. Simpson, June 26, 1995.
2. Author interview of John Rother, April 1, 1994.
3. *Story of AARP*, Margaret Abrams, AARP-produced history, 1971; also AARP Oral History interview of Leonard Davis, April 12, 1988.
4. The letter was published in the *NRTA Journal*, June 1957, as "NRTA Insurance Plan: A Trail-Blazing Report."

5. *Story of AARP.*

6. "Stipulation in the Matter of Applications and/or Licenses of Leonard Davis, Respondent," State of New York Insurance Department, Richard E. Stewart, Superindendent of Insurance, two pages, signed August 13, 1969; *The AARP: America's Most Powerful Lobby and the Clash of Generations*, Charles R. Morris, Times Books, 1996.

7. AARP oral history interview of Ruth Lana, January 11, 1988.

8. *Harriet V. Miller v. Leonard Davis, Lloyd I. Singer, Alfred Miller, Cyril F. Brickfield and Colonial Penn Group, Inc.*, filed in the Superior Court of the District of Columbia, May 2, 1978.

9. Letter, Alfred Miller of Miller, Singer, Raives & Brandes to James A. Maigret, Director, Financial Operations & Planning Office, AARP, November 5, 1987.

10. "Personal Memorandum," W.L. Mitchell memo to Bernard E. Nash regarding "AARP Board Meeting February 8-9, 1973," February 28, 1973.

11. Confidential memorandum of Alice VanLandingham to fellow Board members, June 12, 1976.

12. AARP oral history interview of Eugene Thrift, December 6, 1988.

13. Harriet Miller lawsuit.

14. Fitch oral history interview.

15. Author interview of Lloyd Wright, January 16, 1996.

16. AARP oral history interview of David Jeffreys, May 5, 1989.

17. AARP oral history interview of Mary Chenoweth, Area III staffer, June 12, 1991.

18. Morton Mintz, *Washington Post*, January 3, 1979.

19. Irwin Landau, editor, Consumer Reports, memorandum to Rhoda H. Karpatkin, January 7, 1976.

20. Landau letter to Andrew A. Rooney, *60 Minutes*, November 23, 1977.

21. "Bedmates: Colonial Penn Group and the AARP have an unusual relationship—you might even call it incestuous," *Forbes*, February 1, 1976, 2.

22. "Feds Probe Retiree Group," Jack Anderson and Les Whitten, October 13, 1977.
23. Morton Mintz, *Washington Post*, January 3, 1979.
24. *AARP News Bulletin*, March 1979, 1.
25. *AARP News Bulletin*, March 1979, 1.

CHAPTER 7

1. Letter to author, March 29, 1994.
2. Letter to author, May 9, 1994.
3. "Member Services," part of a series called "Where We Stand: AARP's Views on Important Issues," December 1991.
4. "Empire builders," Richard Phalon, *Forbes*, February 22, 1988.
5. "For AARP, a Reversal of Fortune," Elizabeth Mehren and Robert A. Rosenblatt, *Los Angeles Times*, August 22, 1995.
6. Quoted in "Old Money," Christopher Georges, *Washington Monthly*, June 1992.
7. *Consumer Reports*, January 1976—the article that began the break with Colonial Penn insurance. However, the observation is still accurate twenty years later.
8. Quoted in "Should AARP Handle Your Finances?," *Money*, October 1988.
9. Class Action Complaint, *Joseph H. Schiff, on his own behalf and on behalf of all other persons similarly situated* vs. *American Association of Retired Persons*, Civil Action No. 613-95.
10. Written testimony of M. Roy Goldberg of the Washington D.C.–based law firm, Galland, Kharasch, Morse & Garfinkle. Prepared May 25, 1995, for appearance before the U.S. Senate Finance Committee, Subcommittee on Social Security and Family Policy.
11. Order, Superior Court of the District of Columbia, Civil Division, *Joseph Schiff, et al.* v. *American Association of Retired Persons*, signed in chambers May 3, 1995, by Geoffrey M. Alprin, Associate Judge.
12. Letter to author, March 24, 1994.
13. Letter to author, June 3, 1994.

14. "Marketing and Lobbying," *National Journal*, October 24, 1987.

15. Quoted in "Senior Schism," Marilyn Werber Serafini, *National Journal*, May 6, 1995.

16. Author interview, June 26, 1995.

17. "Whose Side Are They On, Anyway?," Ron Suskind, *Smart Money*, February 1993.

18. "Whose Side Are They On, Anyway?," ibid.

19. "Health Care Reform," speech, Bruce Vladeck, 1994 AARP Biennial Convention, Anaheim, California, May 4, 1994.

20. "Nonprofit Status Comes Under Scrutiny," David S. Hilzenrath, *Washington Post*, May 22, 1995; also *Associated Press* report, June 4, 1995.

21. Interviews with author associate Melinda Maas, July 8 and August 8, 1994.

22. "Report to the Board of Directors from the Board Committee on Membership and Member Services," Second Committee Meeting, March 14–15, 1994.

23. Membership Division Monthly Report to the Executive Director, May 1994.

24. Ibid, June 1994.

25. Ibid, September 1994.

26. "Business and Financial Practices of the AARP." Hearings before the Subcommittee on Social Security and Family Policy, June 20, 1995, 62–3.

27. "AARP Flexes Its Muscle," Frank Swoboda, *Washington Post*, April 18, 1988.

28. "The Formidable Threat of AARP's Credit Union," Michael P. Sullivan, *The American Banker*, September 15, 1988.

29. "Retirees Vaunted Credit Union Flops," William Jackson, *Business First–Columbus*, March 26, 1990.

30. Author interview, June 23, 1994.

31. AARP oral history interview, January 4, 1988.

32. *National Retired Teachers Association Journal*, March 1958.

33. Jeremy Main, *Money*, March 1975; Frances Cerra, *New York Times*, December 29, 1975; *Consumer Reports*, January 1976.

34. "Songs for the Happy Travelers," AARP Travel Service, 4th print-ing, July 1968. Its introduction reads: "On the moon-drenched deck of an ocean liner... on a sleek-soaring jet... or in the com-fortable interior of a bus... these songs will give a lift to the AARP traveler."

35. AARP oral history interview, May 21, 1990.

CHAPTER 8

1. Letter to Author, March 21, 1994.

2. Letter to Author, April 27, 1994.

3. AARP oral history interview of Leonard Davis, April 12, 1988.

4. Partly because of ongoing litigation, Haft rarely grants inter-views. However, he did reminisce with the author about his involvement with the AARP, October 29, 1996.

5. *Journal of the National Retired Teachers Association*, September 1962.

6. "Member Services Tracking Study, 1987," AARP Planning and Analysis department, "Confidential," April 1988, 78, 84.

7. Letter to author, March 30, 1994.

8. AARP oral history interview of Francisco Carranco, AARP board member and treasurer, June 13, 1991.

9. Letter from F. Nicholas Willard, Director, Governmental Affairs, Retired Persons Services, to Rep. Ronnie G. Flippo, Chairman, Subcommittee on Select Revenue Measures, Ways and Means Committee, U.S. House of Representatives, June 17, 1987.

10. Membership Division Monthly Report, February 1996.

11. Ibid, April 1996.

12. As reported in "Ouch!: Which hurts more, the shot or the bill?," John Greenwald, *Time*, March 8, 1993, 53–5.

13. "Why Drugs Cost More in U.S.," Gina Kolata, *New York Times*, May 24, 1991.

14. "Prescription Drug Pricing Hurting the Poor, Elderly," Sara Fritz, *Los Angeles Times*, January 30, 1994.

15. Interview with author, June 22, 1995.

16. Interview with author, June 5, 1995.

17. "Lovers and haters of mail Rx service debate at symposium," Martha Glaser, *Drug Topics*, April 21, 1986, 26.
18. "Inside mail-order pharmacy operations," Judy Chi, *Drug Topics*, January 19, 1987, 22.
19. "Safety and Soundness Standards in the Mail Order Prescription Industry," hearings.
20. Public Policy Agenda, official AARP legislative positions, April 1995, 190–91.
21 . "The anti-mail order drive: Could it backfire?", Bill Robinson, *Drug Topics*, November 3, 1986, 16.
22. Letter, John M. Rector, Esq., Vice President of Government Affairs & General Counsel, NARD, to Commissioner David A. Kessler, Food and Drug Administration, March 29, 1991.
23. Letter to author, March 28, 1994.
24. "Under the AARP Umbrella: Responses to Frequently Asked Questions about AARP," AARP Membership Communications Department, March 1995.
25. "1994 Member Services Quality Study,"40–1.
26. Interview with author, June 29, 1995.

CHAPTER 9

1. "Good Nutrition," speech given by Jane Brody at the 1994 AARP Biennial Convention in Anaheim, California, May 3, 1994.
2. Letter to author, March 19, 1994.
3. "1994 Annual Summary Report—Member Correspondence," Anita Salustro, Membership Communications Department, March 30, 1995.
4. Horace Deets, August 26, 1994, letter to the editor, *Washington Post.*
5. Letter to author, March 28, 1994.
6. Letter to Betty Fowler from Joe Bielec, Manager, AARP Enrollment Division, The Prudential Insurance Company of America, March 2, 1993.
7. Testimony of Dr. John Lione, member, AARP Board of Directors, before the House Committee on Ways and Means, Subcommittee on Health, September 29, 1994.

8. Welch and others were speaking at a March 1989 forum the APA convened to examine this emerging drug problem.

9. Lione testimony, citing a 1992 review article in Drugs & Aging which found that between 3 percent and 11 percent of hospital admissions could be attributed to adverse drug reactions caused by mismedication.

10. "Harper's Index," *Harper's* magazine, December 1986, citing as its source a book, *The American Forecaster 1987*; also "First, Do No Harm," Ellen Ruppel Shell, *Atlantic*, May 1988, 83–4. It should be noted that an unknown number of the prescription drug deaths are deliberate, suicidal drug overdoses.

11. Statistic cited in "Harper's Index," *Harper's*, October 1992, 15.

12. Quoted in *AARP News Bulletin* article, "Unlike 'birds of a feather,' some drugs don't go together," Peggy Eastman, March 1989. Wolfe is also co-author of the book, *Worst Pills, Best Pills: The Older Adult's Guide to Avoiding Drug-Induced Death or Illness.*

13. Interview with author, June 5, 1995; also quoted in "America's 'other drug problem' overwhelms thousands, experts say," Peggy Eastman, *AARP News Bulletin*, April 1989, 1, 3.

14. "Over one-third surveyed report drug reactions," *AARP News Bulletin*, December 1984, 11.

15. "Good Nutrition," May 3, 1994.

16. The Oraflex story was told in author interviews and the following publications: "Government Says Deaths Related to Arthritis Drug Now at Eight," Betty Anne Williams, *Associated Press*, July 30, 1982; "Arthritis Drug Stirs Ban Effort," *Washington Post*, July 31, 1982; "Retiree Group Warns About Oraflex," *Associated Press*, July 31, 1982; "Manufacturer Voluntarily Suspends Sale of Oraflex," *AARP News Bulletin*, September 1982, 3; "Pharmacy Service Alerts Doctors on Oraflex Dosage," *AARP News Bulletin*, September 1982, 8; "Release of Dangerous Drugs Draws Fire," *AARP News Bulletin*, January 1983, 2; "FDA Approves Limited Use of Oraflex at Lilly's Request," *AARP News Bulletin*, March 1983, 13; "Oraflex Campaign Is Called Misleading," *AARP News*

Bulletin, March 1984, 2; "Bitter pills," Francesca Lunzer, *Forbes,* June 3, 1985, 203; "Miracle Drugs or Media–Drugs?"*Consumer Reports,* March 1992, 144–46.

17. "Bitter pills".
18. "Drugs fighting drugs posing growing threat," January 1994.
19. Lione testimony, September 20, 1994.
20. "Tranquilizers Make Zombies of Elderly, Council Charges," Jack Anderson Merry-Go-Round, Bell-McClure Syndicate, November 15, 1970.
21. "Overdosing the Elderly," Christine Gorman, *Time,* August 8, 1994, 47; "For 1 in 4 Elderly, an Improper Drug," *U.S. News & World Report,* August 8, 1994.
22. Medications and the Elderly, 203; "Estrogen roller coaster," Robin Marantz Henig, *AARP Bulletin,* February 1990, 2; *The Pill Book,* 312–318, "Estrogen: friend or foe?", Susan L. Crowley, *AARP Bulletin,* June 1994, 2, 5.

CHAPTER 10

1. "A Management Study of the Communications of the American Association of Retired Persons," conducted by outside consultants, Chester Burger & Co., Inc., September 1985.
2. "A Management Study...."
3. After nearly two decades with AARP, the past nine years as head of the Membership Division, Haefer resigned from AARP in May 1997.
4. Author interview of John Rother, April 1, 1994.
5. 1994 AARP Awareness Study, Claude A. Rankin, Developmental Services Department, August 1994, stamped "Confidential"; also, confidential AARP "Stratogram," entitled, "Why Members Join and Why Members Lapse," Spring 1995.
6. Author interview of John Rother, June 29, 1995.
7. Author interview of Lloyd Wright, January 16, 1996.
8. "A Management Study...."
9. Lamberson letter to author, April 11, 1994.
10. Primarily an extrapolation from "Direct Mail Results Summary,"

May 18, 1995, a full accounting of all pieces of mail sent from January to April 1995.

11. "Direct mail is king," *American Salesman*, July 1996, 3.

12. "Membership Division Monthly Report," May 1996.

13. United Press International stories, October 23 and 24, 1985.

14. 1994 Demographic Analysis, prepared by India Walsh, Developmental Services Department, Membership Division, February 1995; also 1992 Membership Demographics Study, prepared by Ella D. Cameron, Developmental Services Department, September 1992.

15. "Strategic Issues," Stratogram #12, planning document, 13 pages, April 1995.

16. Letter to author, March 30, 1994.

17. However, California is the state with the most members—more than three million, according to Horace Deets during an October 19, 1995, America Online chat.

18. Letter to author, April 1, 1994.

19. Letter to author, April 8, 1994.

20. Author interview of Richard Henry, April 7, 1994.

21. "AARP's $8 bargain...."

22. The official added of the game project, "the whole thing was ridiculous. We used it for one meeting, when it was first introduced. I don't know that it's been used since." He suggested the greater insult was the waste of money the game's creation represented.

23. "AARP Volunteer Census," Confidential, November 1994, prepared by Office of Volunteer Coordination, AARP.

24. Charles Morris, *AARP book*, 7–9.

25. Author interview, May 11, 1995.

26. "Members Respond to Block Money Market Adversaries," *AARP News Bulletin*, October 1981, 3.

27. "Revisions to AARP Chapter Handbook," *Highlights*, January 1990, 13.

28. "Responsibilities to AARP: Representation," "Volunteer Policies of the American Association of Retired Persons," approved by the Board of Directors, June 1991, 10; reviewed and amended June 1993.

29. Series of letters and newsletters sent by Walker in late 1988 to Jack Carlson, a Republican who had been fired as AARP Executive Director.
30. Letter to author, April 1, 1994. "My own struggle, to keep my name off the obituary page, takes priority and precludes continued opposition," he wrote. "When my present membership expires, I do not intend to renew."
31. Letter to author, April 11, 1994.
32. "Texas City Revises Hiring Policy After AARP Chapter Protest," *AARP News Bulletin*, November 1975, 1.

CHAPTER 11

1. Letter to author, mailed April 9, 1994. He explained: "I am a former member of the organization, but I quit in disgust. It seems the exclusive goal of the organization is to get more of something-for-nothing from the federal government. 'Give us this, give us that, give us more!' I worked harder than I really cared for what I earned, and I know the younger workers have to work even harder to support the senior population at their present level of prosperity."
2. Letter to author, March 18, 1994.
3. As quoted in "A New Pitch to Aging Baby Boomers: Marketers Rewriting Rules for Generation That Sees Itself Getting Older but Not Old," *Washington Post*, September 16, 1995.
4. Letter to author, March 29, 1994.
5. Minutes of Board Committee on Membership and Member Services, March 15, 1994.
6. Interview with author, July 19, 1995.
7. "Strategic Issues," Stratogram #12, April 1995.
8. Interview with author, August 12, 1996.

CHAPTER 12

1. Letter to the author, April 2, 1994.
2. As quoted in "The World According to AARP," Lee Smith, *Fortune*, February 29, 1988.

3. The free spouse advantage annoys single members because it requires them to pay more than a married individual. Sue Carol Cox of Beckley, West Virginia, wrote a letter to the author, May 9, 1994: "If I pay $5 for membership, and you pay $5 for membership, that is equality, correct? But if I pay $5 for membership, and you pay $2.50 that is in-equality. AARP, like a few other organizations in our country, penalizes the single person, male, female, widowed, divorced, etc. If a man/or woman pays for membership, his/her 'SPOUSE' pays only half the amount. My final complaint about AARP: they won't even listen to someone voicing their opinion."

4. Letter to author, June 6, 1994.

5. "Why Members Join and Why Members Lapse," planning document, Stratogram #26, April 1995.

6. Membership Division Monthly Report to the Executive Director, May 1994.

7. United Press International, December 5, 1985; "Association celebrates milestone by honoring 20 millionth member," *AARP News Bulletin*, January 1986, 1; "Executive Director's Report," Cyril Brickfield, *AARP News Bulletin*, February 1986, 8.

8. Interview with author, March 8, 1994.

9. Interview with author, June 6, 1995.

10. As quoted in *Direct*, November 1994.

11. "AARP dues increase first in 10 years," *AARP Bulletin*, March 1992, 3.

12. "Why Members Join and Why Members Lapse," Stratogram #26, April 1995.

13. Letter to author, April 14, 1994.

14. Letter to author, March 21, 1994.

15. Letter to author, April 13, 1994.

16. "Strategic Issues," Stratogram #12, April 1995.

APPENDIX A

1. "Our Rating for AARP's Deals: A Middling C+," *Money* press release, June 12, 1995; also "Taking A Hard Look At AARP's Deals."

2. Included in this figure is $17.7 million that AARP earned in interest while floating the $3 billion-plus in premium checks in various banks, before consigning the money to Prudential.

3. Letter to author, April 25, 1994.

4. See "Long-Term Care: Why you should pass up this subpar coverage," *Money*, July 1995.

5. Recounted in "Whose Side Are They On, Anyway?"

6. Letter to author, April 26, 1994.

7. Letter to author, April 28, 1994.

8. Letter to author, April 14, 1994.

9. Letter to author, March 28, 1994.

10. Membership Division Monthly Report to the Executive Director, January 1994.

11. Ibid, February, March, and April 1996.

12. Ibid, April 1996.

13. AARP Awareness Study, August 1994.

14. During 1995, members rented 528,851 cars from Avis, National, and Hertz, according to the Membership Division Monthly Report to the Executive Director, March 1996. "Car rental companies earned over $104 million in revenue from these rentals; royalties paid to the association totaled $5.2 million, a 14 percent increase over 1994."

15. Letter to author, March 23, 1994.

16. Letter to author, March 23, 1994.

17. Letter to author, March 23, 1994.

18. Letter to author, March 31, 1994.

19. Credit card revenue is not determined by how much is borrowed on the card. Instead, it is a combination of interest paid and annual fees (where applicable) which is called ROA, or "Return On Assets." AARP gets 50 percent of the amount by which the ROA exceeds 2.75 percent. Assuming the cards have at least a 3.75 percent return on assets, the total revenue is at least $65.25 million.

20. Ibid, March and August 1996.

21. Membership Division Monthly Report, June 1996.

22. The AARP credit card computer still only gave him a $10,000 credit limit, when he had asked for $25,000, according to an account in *Money* magazine, "Make Sure Visa Will Accept You," John Manners, February 1993.

23. Interview and one-year summary in ten-page confidential AARP credit card list of members denied credit, and reasons for the denials.

24. Membership Division Monthly Reports, May and August 1996.

25. Established in 1919, Scudder is one of America's oldest independent counsel firms for private individuals, and is certainly one of the most respected.

26. The $12 billion was not added to the overall revenue figure at the beginning of this chapter because invested money temporarily consigned to a financial institution or investment firm is not revenue. Only the "management fees" and other charges on the investments is counted as revenue, which is the $83 million figure for 1994. Still, it is a stunning example of membership trust that the annual "cash flow" to AARP and its affiliated businesses annually is in excess of $15 billion.

27. "Materials to Respond to Criticism of AARP," James R. Holland, Memorandum to "All Staff," April 17, 1995.

28. "Model to Develop New Offering/New Products for Non-Profit Organizations," Kathy Hardy, *AARP*, April 1993.

APPENDIX B

1. General information on NCOA from the organization itself, including "Partnering to Shape the Future," 1996. Also author interviews with NCOA official Michael Renemer, October 23, 1996; Earl Kragnes, August 22, 1996; Robert Blancato, Executive Director, White House Conference on Aging, July 18, 1995; and AARP Executive Director Horace Deets, April 1, 1994.

2. "Top Ten Political Slush Funds," Backgrounder, *Heritage Foundation*, March 4, 1996.

3. An excellent book on the early roots of seniors groups, particularly California-based ones, is *Senior Power: Growing Old*

Rebelliously, Paul Kleyman, Glide Publications, 1974. NCSC references are on pages 84 to 87.

4. Quoted in *The Palm Beach Post*, Larry Lipman, August 12, 1994. However, the author interviewed Burns in October 1996.

5. *New York Times*, May 27, 1994—the same press conference at which Sen. Pryor spoke.

6. *The Washington Merry-Go-Round* column, Jack Anderson and Dale Van Atta, April 16, 1990.

7. Author interview, June 13, 1994.

ACKNOWLEDGMENTS

The question that publisher and friend Jeff Carneal posed after lunch seemed awfully interesting: Do you think the leadership of the American Association of Retired Persons (AARP) actually represents its members?

Thus began a four-year odyssey through the puzzling labyrinth of the largest, richest, and most effective lobbying organization in the world, during which I had amassed so much information that, as an anonymous guest at a staff-only AARP "Learning Center Expo," I repeatedly beat out all AARP staff attendees at the "AARP Trivia Quiz" section.

This account would not have been possible without the assistance of the more than seven hundred AARP officials and others I interviewed for this book. Some AARP sources supplied me with thousands of pages of confidential and internal AARP memoranda, surveys, and financial documents. Most prefer to remain anonymous, but of those who went on the record, James O'Maoilearca and Robert Covais deserve special thanks here. Each left the organization during the course of my writing this book, and, sadly, James died in 1997 of cancer. He had so hoped to read this long-awaited account of the AARP.

Reaching AARP's vast membership through non-AARP-approved channels proved challenging. I chose to send a Letter to the Editor to more than 500 American newspapers and many of the editors, graciously, published the letter. The thousands of letters I received contained invaluable insight into their view of an AARP run amok. (In fact, more than 90 percent were negative about AARP's lobbying positions.)

Two outside "heroes" who preceded me in launching charges at the AARP have also earned my respect and thanks. Former Senator Alan Simpson of Wyoming was unflinching in his crusade against AARP's voracious appetite for the federal taxpayer dollar (and so was his capable staff, led by Chuck Blahous).

The second crusader is Paul Hewitt, late of the National Taxpayers Union Foundation. He's one of the fastest analysts in Washington with a quip and quote, using facts that hold up under close scrutiny. Paul kept my spirits up when they flagged, and, just as important, directed a critical financial grant my way from the John M. Olin Foundation.

This book would also not have been possible without help from my friend Daryl Gibson, who was irreplaceable as editor, writer, and manuscript polisher. Also providing significant assistance were Jan Moller, Melinda Maas, Aaron Karp, Ed Henry, Rebecca Walsh, Gayle Worland, and Kathy Kidd. With wit and warmth, my friend Michael Binstein carried me through some of the rougher seas as this project spread beyond the horizon and seemed unending, as did my mentors, columnist Jack Anderson and *Reader's Digest* Executive Editor William Schulz.

I would also like to thank the team at Regnery Publishing, including Al Regnery, who caught Carneal's vision of the book, and editors Harry Crocker and Erica Rogers, without whom this book would never have happened.

Finally, I am deeply indebted to my wife, Lynne, and my three children, Tara, Dylan, and Kate for thier support and sacrifice. They suffered inattention and worse as the information gathering dragged on. Softball games weren't attended, vacations were canceled, and "shared sacrifice" was required once the advance was eaten up early in the project.

And now, at the end of the day, I am mindful that my father Bruce was a first-rate editor himself, a talent he employed cleaning up the reports of captains and admirals under whom he served in the U.S. Navy. He died in 1989; I miss his curmudgeonly but insightful criticism.

My mother Vera is seventy-three years old now, an indefatigable, independent-minded Renaissance woman. She's authored two fine manuscripts of her own while running a thriving bed-and-breakfast called "10,000 Delights" on Keuka Lake in upstate New York. It was she who inspired me to finish this work.

—*Dale Van Atta*
Washington, D.C.
November 1997

INDEX

A

AARP: budget, 14; formal beginning of, 51; New York World's Fair-exhibit, 52; organizations competing with, 163–167; percentage of staff eligible for membership, 20; restructuring and downsizing efforts, 23; revenue sources, 14–15; taxability of, 14. *See also* Board of Directors

AARP Bulletin: downsizing article, 23–24; new building article, 30

AARP Drug Buying Service, 88

AARP Federal Credit Union, 81–83, 157

AARP Financial Services Corporation, 159–160

AARP Learning Center, 46

F

G

increase in IRS audits, 16; liberal causes, 16–17, 52; Medigap insurance, 77–79; membership decline and, 139–140; opposition to and membership decline, 146–147; Seniors Coalition, 166–167; size of AARP and, 13, 14; state lobbying efforts, 125–126; volunteers and, 123–126; write-in and call-in campaigns to Congress, 124–125

Lodging discounts, 155–157

Loftus, Bob, 82

Long-distance telephone calling minutes free for members, 140

Long-term care insurance, 151

Los Angeles Times, AARP membership dues as revenue source, 74

Louisiana, pharmacy service licensing, 99

Low, Juliette, 47

M

Mack, P.A., 81

Magaziner, Ira, 79

Maigret, James, 23

Mail-order pharmacy service: AARP's answer to criticism of, 102, 103; adverse drug reactions and, 114; antitrust hearings on high pharmaceutical prices, 88–89; average age and income of members and, 103; beginnings, 87–88; community pharmacies and, 96–101, 114; drug price inflation effect, 95–96; Eli Lilly Company and, 95; fraudulent prescriptions and, 99; generic products, 91, 96; government promotion of, 100–101; Haft's involvement, 88–89; health care reform and, 17; McHugh's involvement, 89–92; Member Choice card, 94–95; member dissatisfaction, 101–102; mismedication possibility, 114; Mitchell bill and, 106–107; National Council on Aging, 163; no prepayment requirement feature, 90; nonprescription products, 90–91, 98; nonprofit status, 92, 94; number of customers, 94; percentage of market controlled by, 87; prescription drug instructions and, 97–98; prescription errors and, 99–100; property and sales taxes and, 98; Retired Persons Services, Inc., and, 92–94, 103; RPS board oversight, 93; safety concerns, 97; savings reports of members, 101–103; state regulation and, 98–99; telemarketing, 92, 114; time-saving measures, 91

Mann, Gladys, 153

Marriott hotels, 155–156

Maryland Pharmaceutical Association, 89

R

S